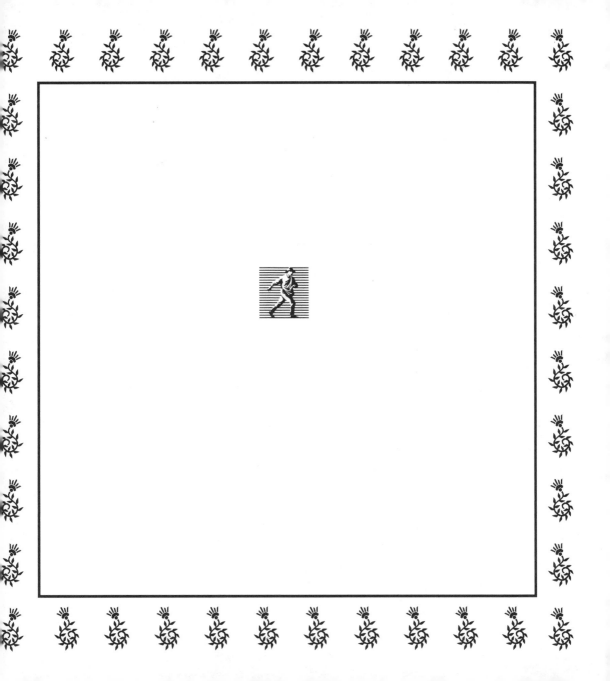

Also by Ceri Hadda:

Coffee Cakes

CERI HADDA

SIMON & SCHUSTER

New York London Toronto Sydney Tokyo Singapore

CUPCAKES

SIMON & SCHUSTER
Rockefeller Center
1230 Avenue of the Americas
New York, New York 10020

Copyright © 1995 by Ceri Hadda

SIMON & SCHUSTER and colophon are registered trademarks
of Simon & Schuster Inc.

Designed by Bonni Leon-Berman
Manufactured in the United States of America

1 3 5 7 9 10 8 6 4 2

Library of Congress Cataloging-in-Publication Data
Hadda, Ceri.
Cupcakes / Ceri Hadda.
p.   cm.
Includes index.
1. Cake.   I. Title.
TX771.H234   1995   94-30275
641.8′653—dc20   CIP
ISBN: 0-671-86436-X

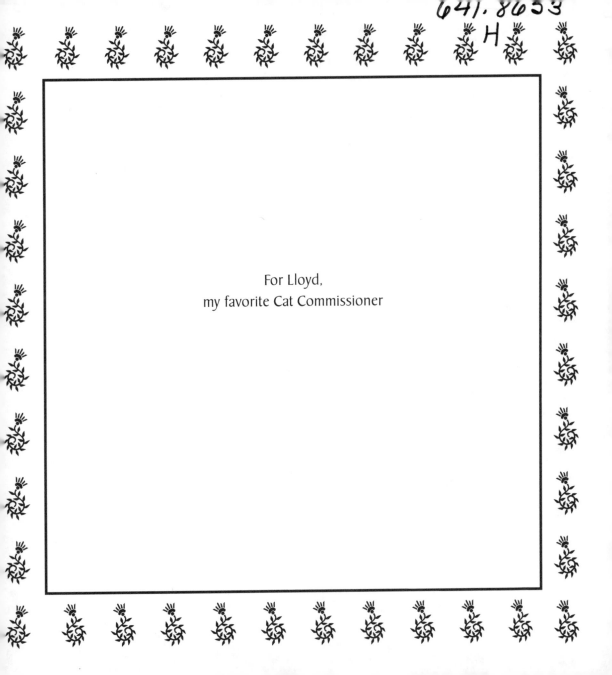

For Lloyd,
my favorite Cat Commissioner

Acknowledgments

Every cookbook author cherishes the help of tasters, testers, readers, and those whose mere encouragement provides the energy to put yet another pan in the oven.

Once again, thanks to Jane Dystel, for representing me and finding my manuscript a good home.

Thanks to Syd Miner for bringing the book to fruition.

Thanks to Kathy Hadda, Jessica Feinleib, and Anne Wright for testing, testing, testing beyond the call of duty.

Thanks to Nick Malgieri and Richard Sax for their knowledgeable advice.

Thanks to the Alkire and Kunicki families; Robin Schiff, George and Caroline Anesi; Susan, Michael, and Sam Barnes; Mary Caldwell, Matt Caputo, and Angela Caputo; Diane Dermarderosian; Jim Fobel; Lloyd Gelwan; Annemarie Hadda; Janet Hadda and Allan Tobin; Jackie Hollywood; Keren Osman and John Krinsky; Miriam Osman; Bonnie Seligson; Mike Slattery; Pam Smith; Susan Solomon; Beth Stephenson; Charles Wright and Andrew Zerman for tasting, tasting, tasting beyond the call of duty.

Thanks to Marie T. Walsh for teaching me the ins and outs of recipe development and writing.

Finally, thanks to members of the Mount Sinai School of Medicine Class of 1996 for their comments, suggestions, and insatiable hunger.

Contents

Introduction

Say the word "cupcake" and watch a smile emerge. For most Americans, the cupcake is as quintessential a culinary experience as Proust's madeleine. Moist and springy, topped with a generous swirl of frosting or a lustrous glaze, this is the children's treat that nobody is too old to enjoy.

Cupcakes are fun. Their youthful associations run the gamut of Americana, from school and church bake sales to birthday parties and after-school snacks. Their single-serving size makes them uniquely portable and tremendously appealing. There's something about having a little cake *all* to yourself!

Cupcakes are simple. The batter is usually made in one bowl, spooned into muffin pans, and baked in less than half an hour. Most recipes can be accomplished with just a bowl or two, a hand mixer, and one muffin-pan set. Decoration can be as easy as a dusting of confectioners' sugar, a flourish of frosting, or a quick glaze. Even additional embellishments—a cherry, a glazed walnut, multicolored sprinkles—seldom require skill or time. Finally, especially with the use of paper cupcake liners, cleanup is a snap. What could be *less* daunting than preparing a batch?

Cupcakes are adaptable. Despite—or perhaps because of—their simplicity, they can be varied in countless ways to fit occasions formal and informal, funky and traditional, everyday and celebratory. In addition to basic cupcake recipes, sections on frosting and decorating ideas will inspire unique combinations that personalize every batch.

Basic Cupcake Ingredients and Techniques

INGREDIENTS

Although most cupcakes aren't fancy concoctions, they still should be made from high-quality ingredients.

B u t t e r. I bake exclusively with *unsalted (or "sweet") butter*, a baking basic I learned from my mother. Salted butter is unpredictable: Because of the salt, which acts as a preservative, it may have been lying around the store longer than it should; but if that is what you have on hand, reduce or eliminate the salt called for in the recipe.

Never use whipped or light butter, because they contain added water and air not accounted for in a recipe.

Since butter and margarine have the same amount of calories, the only reason to use the latter in baking is to reduce cholesterol and save a few pennies. Personally, I find the occasional indulgence of butter well worth the guilt!

Butter freezes well, so I buy large quantities on sale and store them in the freezer. Most of the 1-pound packages are already wrapped in plastic, which makes the butter less likely to pick up "off" flavors from the freezer. At 0 degrees Fahrenheit or lower, butter keeps well for up to nine months.

Milk. I always bake with fresh whole milk, never ultrapasteurized or ultra-high-temperature (UHT)-processed. The latter two methods subject the milk to temperatures that give it a "cooked" flavor.

Sour Cream and Yogurt. Although yogurt is perceivably more tangy and less creamy than sour cream, it can be substituted ounce for ounce for sour cream in any of my cupcake recipes. Obviously, the added fat associated with sour cream will make a cake extra tender and moist. Nonetheless, the presence of other ingredients, such as butter and eggs, usually benefits the cake's texture, too.

This year, I discovered the joys of yogurt cheese. Made with plain low-fat yogurt drained in an inexpensive mesh cone or a coffee filter, it can be used as a tangy topping for cupcakes: Stir in a bit of sugar and vanilla, spread on top of cupcakes, then garnish with fresh berries and an additional sifting of sugar or with powdered vanilla, if desired.

Keep both sour cream and yogurt refrigerated until just before you will be using them. Never freeze them, since they'll separate.

Heavy or Whipping Cream. Always buy cream from a reliable source where you know it's been kept under constant refrigeration. Once you get it home, immediately place it in the refrigerator, where it should keep for at least a week. Do not freeze cream; its texture will be altered.

Whenever possible, I use fresh, rather than ultrapasteurized, cream, although I don't notice as marked a difference here as I do between fresh and UHT milk.

Buttermilk. Buttermilk adds a tender, tangy quality to cupcakes. Although its rich-sounding moniker refers to its original role as a byproduct of butter making, today's commercially available buttermilk has no butter in it at all; in fact, its fat profile is more similar to that of skim milk.

Buttermilk can be kept refrigerated for up to two weeks. If you're an infrequent user of buttermilk, the powdered variety, now widely available across the country, is a perfect substitute. Or, add a teaspoon or two of lemon juice or vinegar to a cup of milk, and let it stand until it curdles and sours.

Eggs. All recipes in this book have been created and tested using room-temperature *extra-large eggs*. If you're substituting eggs of a different size, a handy rule of thumb is: 1 large egg = 2 ounces (¼ cup); 1 extra-large egg = 2¼ ounces; and 1 jumbo egg = 2½ ounces. Buy clean, uncracked Grade A or AA eggs from refrigerated cases. Once you get home, refrigerate the eggs immediately and keep them refrigerated until you'll be using them. Do not store eggs in the egg shelf of your refrigerator door; they will be subject to repeated temperature fluctuations and breakage. Instead, keep the eggs in the cartons in which you bought them, which also inhibits the absorption of refrigerator odors.

• You can store whole eggs in the refrigerator for four to five weeks beyond the pack date. All the recipes in this book use room-temperature eggs. If you are not using them for baking, always keep them refrigerated until just before you'll be using them. (When a recipe uses room-temperature eggs, thirty minutes out of the refrigerator should suffice); room-temperature eggs age seven times as quickly as those kept under refrigeration.

- Store egg whites in a tightly closed container in the refrigerator for up to four days.
- Store unbroken egg yolks in water to cover in a tightly closed container in the refrigerator. Use within a day or two.
- Never freeze whole eggs in their shells.
- To freeze egg yolks, stir ⅛ teaspoon salt or 1½ teaspoons sugar or corn syrup into every four yolks, noting which you've added on a label.
- To freeze whole eggs, beat them together just until blended before pouring into the freezer container.
- To freeze egg whites, no special treatment is needed, though for easier measuring, the whites can be frozen in ice cube trays, unmolded, and stored in plastic freezer bags.
- To thaw frozen eggs, whites, or yolks, refrigerate overnight or place closed container under running cold water. Use the yolks or whole eggs at once. Let the egg whites sit at room temperature for about 30 minutes, if you'll be whipping them.

C r e a m   C h e e s e . Whenever possible, I use natural cream cheese free of gums and other additives; not surprisingly, it has a lighter, less "gummy" texture. Whipped cream cheese, aerated to make it fluffy, is not suitable for recipes in this book.

Buy only as much cream cheese as you'll be using for a particular recipe, since it does not keep well. Never freeze the cheese.

O i l . For baking, I use corn oil or a flavorless blend, such as Wesson. If desired, nut oils such as walnut, almond, and hazelnut can be substituted for part of the vegetable oil called for in some of the cupcake recipes.

S u g a r . I always have granulated, light and dark brown, and confectioners' sugars on hand.

Since I bake frequently, and since granulated sugar lasts indefinitely, I buy five-pound bags and transfer the sugar to a large glass jar once I've opened the bag. Before making your purchase, check to see that there are few lumps in the sugar; they'll be a nuisance come baking time.

Brown sugar adds a deep, molasses flavor as well as moisture to batters. Most of the recipes using brown sugar in this book call for either light or dark, but you can interchange them or use a combination. Before you buy either sugar, gently squeeze the package to ensure that the sugar is moist. Once you've opened a package, wrap the remainder in a second plastic bag. Rock-hard brown sugar can be softened with a brief stint in a 300-degree oven or the microwave, but the sugar must be used at once or it will reharden. You can also grate the sugar with a hand grater, although it will not provide the same moist results.

Confectioners' (10X) sugar is used as a base for glazes and frostings, as well as dusted onto cupcakes that need no more elaborate treatment than that. If it seems lumpy, sift it before measuring and using it.

Honey and Maple Syrup/Maple Sugar. For general baking, I use an all-purpose blend of honey, one that is mild enough to harmonize with the other ingredients. To minimize crystallization, honey should be stored in an airtight container in a cool place, and in the refrigerator for long-term storage. If it *does* crystallize, place the jar of honey in a saucepan of hot water and heat until the crystals have liquefied.

For baking, I use an amber-colored Grade A maple syrup that is pure but not so strong that it will overpower the other ingredients in my recipe. I always keep opened contain-

ers of maple syrup in the refrigerator, since they tend to go moldy if they're left out too long. Maple sugar, though expensive, lends an autumnal flavor to cakes and frostings. It can be substituted in whole or in part for brown sugar in a recipe.

Flour, All-Purpose. Unless otherwise noted, the recipes in this book use *bleached all-purpose flour.* Since it's presifted, I measure it straight out of the package, first aerating it to remove any isolated lumps, then gently scooping it up with a measuring cup and leveling it across the top of the cup with a table knife.

Flour, Whole-Wheat. Whole-wheat flour adds a nutty flavor and a nice "chew" to some cupcakes. I like buying stone-ground whole-wheat flour because of its pronounced flavor and texture. In hot weather, or if you won't be using up the flour for a while, refrigerate or freeze it, to avoid rancidity.

Leaveners. Baking soda and baking powder give cupcakes their oomph! Store them in a cool, dry place. Since they should be of optimum freshness for best leavening action, replace them often, especially if you live in a warm, humid climate.

All recipes in this book use double-acting baking powder.

Chocolate and Cocoa. As is evidenced by the number of chocolate recipes in this book, I'm mad about chocolate. Since all chocolate keeps almost indefinitely if it's stored in a cool, dark place, I always have a supply of unsweetened and semisweet chocolates on hand, as well as a tin of good-quality unsweetened cocoa powder.

Unsweetened chocolate is available in 1-ounce squares.

For most of my semisweet-, milk-, and white-chocolate needs, I buy 3-ounce bars of Swiss chocolate or use one of the many good-quality brands of chocolate pieces available at the supermarket. Mini-size chips are especially convenient for baking cupcakes and sprinkling on top of frosting for a quick garnish.

Never buy presweetened cocoa powder, only the unsweetened variety. Sift it before measuring if it is lumpy. For recipes in this book, I've used regular cocoa, not the milder, somewhat darker, "Dutched" or alkalized variety.

Don't be alarmed if chocolate turns white upon storage; that's just the cocoa butter coming to the surface in a "bloom." The chocolate is still perfectly usable.

The microwave is an ideal aid in melting chocolate for recipes, whether they are traditionally baked or finished in the microwave.

(In a pinch, 3 tablespoons of unsweetened cocoa and 1 tablespoon of solid vegetable shortening can be used instead of a 1-ounce square of unsweetened chocolate.)

TO MELT CHOCOLATE SQUARES IN THE MICROWAVE

For 1-ounce squares, place 1 square of chocolate, unwrapped, in a completely dry microwavesafe bowl. Heat on medium power for 1½ to 2½ minutes, stirring halfway through cooking time, or until the chocolate is almost melted. (Avoid overcooking the chocolate; it may still hold its shape even though it is already quite soft.) Remove the chocolate from the microwave, then stir it until it melts completely. For 2 squares of chocolate, heat for a total of 3 to 5 minutes. For 3 squares, heat for a total of 4 to 6 minutes.

TO MELT CHOCOLATE CHIPS IN THE MICROWAVE

Place 1 cup (6 ounces) of chips in a completely dry microwavesafe bowl. Heat on medium power for 2 to 4 minutes, stirring after 2 minutes of cooking time, and then every 30 seconds, or until the chocolate is almost melted. (Avoid overcooking the chocolate; the chips may still hold their shape even though they are already quite soft.) Remove the chocolate from the microwave, then stir the chips until they melt completely. For 2 cups (12 ounces) of chips, heat for a total of 4 to 8 minutes.

Cornstarch. Cornstarch adds a silken tenderness to the cupcake batter, and it thickens custards. Remember, just a little goes a long way, so follow recipe amounts carefully.

Salt. Although I like cooking with coarse (kosher) salt, I find regular salt is preferable for baking, since it dissolves more readily.

Nuts. Just-cracked nuts are usually the freshest, but since I rarely have the time to crack my own, nuts in a can or bag from a store with a high turnover suit me just fine. Freeze what you won't use quickly, in tightly closed bags or containers, to avoid rancidity.

Extracts, Flavorings, and Spices. Extracts, flavorings, and spices are used in such small quantities, yet without them, most cupcakes and frostings would taste dull and lackluster. That's why it makes good sense to buy only the finest, purest products available. Never, for example, expect artificial vanilla extract to add the alluring perfume of pure vanilla. (I'm a bit less of a purist, however, when it comes to maple, rum, and coconut extracts; though not totally natural, they still add a nice flavor and scent.)

Powdered vanilla—pure vanilla that's been dried with a touch of sugar—is nice dusted over plain cupcakes or cupcakes that have been topped with whipped cream or yogurt cheese and berries.

With the exception of vanilla and cinnamon, which I find myself using almost every time I bake, I buy flavorings in quantities that I'll be able to use up within a few months. That way, they'll be at their most potent and flavorful when I need them.

Instant espresso powder is a handy flavoring. Just a little bit dissolved in hot water or liqueur makes an intense coffee extract, ready to enhance chocolate, mocha, and coffee batters and glazes.

Store all flavorings in tightly covered containers in a cool, dark place.

Fresh Fruit. While baking is a perfect way to use up slightly overripe fruit, avoid using damaged fruit that is not sound, and plan to eat the cupcakes you bake soon, or store them in the refrigerator or freezer.

TECHNIQUES

Cupcakes are perhaps the simplest of cakes to prepare, as evidenced by the easy techniques used in their preparation.

Whisking. Most of the recipes in this book call for whisking the dry ingredients together rather than the classic sifting technique. A vigorous whirl of the wire whisk quickly combines and delumps flour, leaveners, and spices.

Sifting. Occasionally, as in the case of sponge cupcakes, sifting dry ingredients through a flour sifter or fine sieve provides an extra degree of tenderness and delicacy. I've given instructions for sifting when I think it will improve the final texture of the cupcakes.

Creaming. Creaming is the term used to describe beating butter on its own or with sugar, until it becomes soft and light. Room-temperature (softened) butter is easier to cream than ice-cold butter. Cream butter until it softens and begins to aerate, scraping the sides of the bowl often with a rubber spatula. When sugar is slowly added to the butter as it's creamed, the butter whitens and becomes even lighter in texture.

Chopping Nuts. To chop nuts by hand, place the nuts, a handful at a time, on a clean, dry chopping board. With a heavy chef's knife, cut the nuts into chunks, then continue chopping until the pieces are the size you wish. With a food processor, nuts can be chopped using on-off pulses. Avoid overprocessing, or the nuts will form a paste. One way to minimize this is to add a portion of the sugar called for in the recipe to the nuts in the processor.

TO TOAST NUTS

Toasting nuts enhances their flavor and adds crunch. Place the nuts in a single layer in a roasting pan. Bake at 350 degrees, stirring often, until the nuts are evenly golden and smell fragrant. Watch for burning; the nuts continue to cook from residual heat even when they're removed from the oven.

TO BLANCH NUTS

In the case of hazelnuts, the above toasting method can be taken one step further. Bake the nuts until the skins start to crack and separate from the nuts. Transfer to a tea towel, cover with the towel, and rub vigorously to dislodge as much of the skins as possible. Don't worry if some remain.

For almonds and pistachios, pour boiling water over the nuts in a heatproof bowl; let stand a few minutes, then drain. Working quickly, press the nuts out of their skins; the skins should be loose enough that the nuts pop out of them.

BAKING TIPS

The following tips make cupcake baking even easier.

- The recipes in this book were tested using a standard twelve-tin muffin pan, each tin 3 inches in diameter and 1½ inches high, with a ⅓-cup volume. (The Cupcakes for a Crowd recipes use two 12-tin pans.) A nonstick muffin pan makes for easy unmolding and cleanup, even when paper liners are used.
- Use paper liners: They save time, both in preparing the tins for the cupcake batter and cleaning up after the cupcakes are baked. In addition, cupcakes baked in paper liners rise higher and stay fresh longer. Once, unable to find paper liners, I used some made from aluminum foil and wasn't nearly as happy with the results: The cupcakes over-browned and overbaked.
- For easy pouring of thin batter into muffin tins, transfer the batter to a pitcher with a spout.
- Use two large spoons to "dollop" cupcake batter into tins: one to scoop up the batter, the other to drop it into the tin.
- When baking only one tray of cupcakes, place the tray on the middle oven rack. Rotate the tray in the oven after about two thirds of the baking time, for even baking.
- When baking two trays of cupcakes, place the trays in the upper and lower thirds of the oven. Rotate the trays and switch oven-rack positions after about two thirds of the baking time, for even baking.
- Most of the recipes in this book can be adapted for miniature muffin pans. Use three miniature twelve-tin pans instead of one regular-size pan. Luckily, suitable paper liners are also available, since buttering the tiny pans, unmolding the cupcakes, and cleaning up is three times as tedious as with the regular ones! Smaller amounts of batter bake in less time, so watch the cupcakes closely.
- The frosting and glaze recipes in chapter 9 have been formulated to be just enough

for twelve cupcakes (unless otherwise indicated). In general, about 1½ cups of buttercream or 1 cup of glaze is sufficient for each batch of cupcakes.

- To freeze unfrosted cupcakes, let them cool completely on wire racks, then place them in freezerproof covered containers or in plastic bags.
- To freeze frosted cupcakes, let the cupcakes stand at room temperature until the frosting is no longer tacky. Carefully transfer them to a baking pan or a large freezerproof plate; place them in the freezer until the cupcakes and frosting are frozen. Cover the baking pan or plate tightly with plastic wrap, then with aluminum foil. Alternatively, transfer the frozen cupcakes to a covered freezerproof container. Return to the freezer. To thaw, carefully remove the covering while the frosting is still frozen.
- Cupcakes travel well right in the pan in which they were baked. For picture-perfect results, frost the cupcakes when you reach your destination. Or slice the cupcakes in half crosswise and put a layer of frosting in the middle.
- To frost or glaze cupcakes, spread the topping with a palette knife or butter knife. Or dip the tops of the cupcakes, one at a time, into the bowl of frosting or glaze, swirling as you remove them.
- Cream fillings/frostings can be piped into the centers of cupcakes through the bottoms, using a sharp round tube with the pastry bag. Or pipe the filling on top of the cupcakes in decorative rosettes.

Coffee-Cake Cupcakes

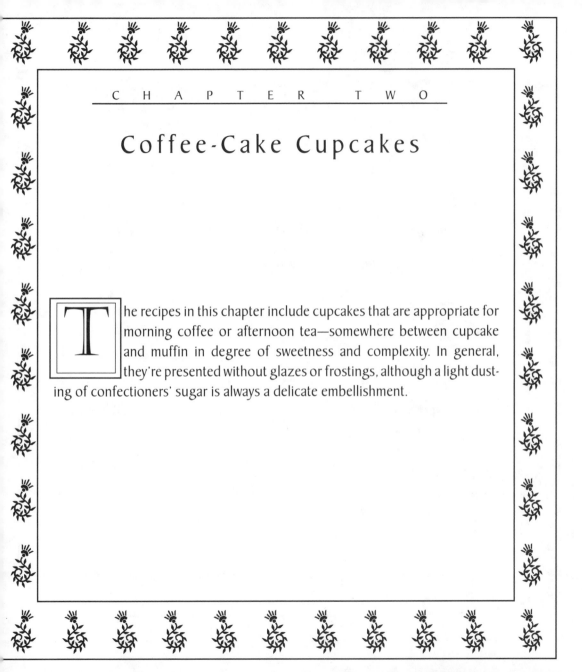

The recipes in this chapter include cupcakes that are appropriate for morning coffee or afternoon tea—somewhere between cupcake and muffin in degree of sweetness and complexity. In general, they're presented without glazes or frostings, although a light dusting of confectioners' sugar is always a delicate embellishment.

Oatmeal–Dried Cherry Cupcakes

Dried cherries, a tangy alternative to raisins, complement this lightly spiced oatmeal batter. Top the cupcakes with Billowy Frosting, tinted pink. Left plain, they're a nice addition to the morning muffin basket.

Makes 12 cupcakes

½ cup old-fashioned oatmeal
¾ cup water
½ cup dried cherries (see Note)
1¼ cups all-purpose flour
1 teaspoon baking powder
½ teaspoon baking soda
½ teaspoon ground cinnamon
¼ teaspoon ground ginger
¼ teaspoon salt

½ cup (1 stick) unsalted butter, softened
¾ cup firmly packed light brown sugar
2 eggs
1 teaspoon pure vanilla extract
¼ teaspoon pure almond extract (optional)
⅓ cup milk

1. Preheat the oven to 350 degrees. Line 12 muffin tins with paper liners or butter and flour the tins; set aside.

2. Place the oatmeal in a medium bowl. In a small saucepan, combine the water and cherries. Bring to a boil over moderate heat; remove from the heat. Pour the cherries into a colander or sieve placed over the oatmeal, stirring the liquid into the oats to moisten evenly. Let the oats and cherries stand while preparing the remainder of the batter.

3. In a medium bowl, whisk together the flour, baking powder, baking soda, cinnamon, ginger, and salt; set aside.

4. In a large bowl, beat the butter until light and fluffy with an electric mixer on high speed. Gradually add the sugar, and continue beating until the mixture is very light and fluffy. Lower the mixer speed to medium. Add the eggs, one at a time, beating well after each addition. Beat in the vanilla extract, almond extract, and oat mixture.

5. Lower the mixer speed to low. Beat in the sifted dry ingredients alternately with the milk, just until combined. Stir in the cherries. The batter will be very sticky.

6. Spoon the batter into the prepared tins.

7. Bake until the cupcakes are golden and springy when lightly pressed with a fingertip, about 20 minutes. Cool in the tins on a wire rack.

Note: Dried cranberries can be substituted for the dried cherries.

DUTCH APPLE CRUNCHCAKES

These nubby cupcakes, loaded with chunks of apple and studded with raisins, are topped with a mantle of cinnamon crumbs. Served warm or at room temperature, they're a treat for breakfast, morning coffee, or afternoon tea—with or without a dusting of confectioners' sugar. For a more elaborate dessert, accompany the crunchcakes with a Calvados-scented custard sauce.

Makes 12 cupcakes

APPLE PIECES
1 large green apple, cut into eighths, each eighth pared, cored, and cut crosswise into 5 or 6 pieces
1 tablespoon sugar
½ teaspoon ground cinnamon

CRUMBS
⅔ cup all-purpose flour
¼ cup firmly packed light brown sugar
¼ cup (½ stick) unsalted butter, softened (or melted, if you're pressed for time)
½ teaspoon ground cinnamon

BATTER
1 cup all-purpose flour
½ teaspoon baking soda
½ teaspoon ground cinnamon
¼ teaspoon salt
⅔ cup sugar
½ cup vegetable oil

1 egg
1 teaspoon pure vanilla extract
2 tablespoons raisins

Confectioners' sugar, for sifting on
the baked cupcakes (optional)

1. Preheat the oven to 350 degrees. Line 12 muffin tins with paper liners or butter and flour the tins; set aside.

2. To prepare the apple pieces, combine the cut-up apple, sugar, and cinnamon in a small bowl, until well blended. Set aside while preparing the rest of the ingredients. Just before using, drain the liquid from the apple pieces, reserving both.

3. To make the crumbs, combine the flour, sugar, butter, and cinnamon in a small bowl until the mixture forms large crumbs. Set aside.

4. To make the batter, whisk together the flour, baking soda, cinnamon, and salt in a small bowl; set aside.

5. In a medium bowl, beat the sugar into the oil with an electric mixer on high. Lower the mixer speed to medium. Beat in the egg, then the vanilla and apple liquid.

6. Lower the mixer speed to low. Beat in the whisked dry ingredients until blended. The batter will be *very* thick and look impossibly gooey—don't despair! Beat in the apples and raisins, breaking up the apples a bit with the mixer. Spoon the batter into the prepared tins.

7. Scatter the crumb mixture over the batter, gently pressing it into the batter.

8. Bake for 30 minutes, or until the crumbs are crisp and the cupcakes are golden brown on top but still seem a bit soft in the center. Turn off the oven. Continue baking for about 5 minutes, or until the cupcakes spring back when gently pressed with a fingertip. Cool the cupcakes in the tins on a wire rack until they are warm or at room temperature. If desired, sift a layer of confectioners' sugar over the cupcakes.

MORNING CUPCAKES

Nuts and cinnamon sugar swirl throughout these little sour cream cupcakes. The final drizzle of melted butter gives them their crunchy topping.

Makes 12 cupcakes

NUTTY CINNAMON SUGAR
1/2 cup finely chopped walnuts or
  pecans
2 tablespoons sugar
1 teaspoon ground cinnamon
1 tablespoon unsalted butter, melted

BATTER
1 cup all-purpose flour
1/2 teaspoon baking powder
1/2 teaspoon baking soda
1/4 teaspoon salt
1/4 cup (1/2 stick) unsalted butter,
  softened
2/3 cup sugar
1 egg
1/2 cup sour cream
1 1/2 teaspoons pure vanilla extract

1. Preheat the oven to 350 degrees. Line 12 muffin tins with paper liners or butter and flour the tins; set aside.

2. To make the nutty cinnamon sugar, combine the nuts, sugar, and cinnamon in a small bowl; set aside. Set aside the melted butter.

3. To make the batter, whisk together the flour, baking powder, baking soda, and salt in a small bowl; set aside.

4. In a medium bowl, beat the butter until light and fluffy with an electric mixer on high speed; gradually beat in the sugar until very light and fluffy. Lower the mixer speed to medium. Beat in the egg, then beat in the sour cream and vanilla. Lower the mixer speed to low. Beat in the flour mixture, just until blended.

5. Pour half of the batter into the prepared muffin tins. Sprinkle with half of the nutty cinnamon sugar. Top with the remaining batter and nut mixture. (Don't worry if the topping is more cinnamon sugar than nuts; this will give the cupcakes extra crunch.) Drizzle with the melted butter. Gently cut through the batter of each cupcake with a table knife two or three times, to swirl the topping through it.

6. Bake until the tops of the cupcakes are golden and crisp, and they are springy when lightly pressed with a fingertip, about 20 minutes. Cool for 15 minutes in the muffin tins on a wire rack.

RASPBERRY CUPCAKES

Because of the highly perishable berries tucked into them, these cupcakes should be served soon after they cool, or else they should be refrigerated or frozen. Top them with orange-flavored whipped cream or with something lemony. Sprinkled with sugar and served plain, they're lovely as very special morning muffins.

Makes 12 cupcakes

1²/₃ cups all-purpose flour
³/₄ cup sugar, plus additional for sprinkling on top of cupcakes, if desired
1 tablespoon baking powder
¼ teaspoon salt
3 eggs

½ cup plus 2 tablespoons (1¼ sticks) unsalted butter, melted and cooled
¼ cup milk
1½ teaspoons pure vanilla extract
½ pint (6 ounces) fresh raspberries, gently rinsed and well drained (about 1¼ cups)

1. Preheat the oven to 350 degrees. Line 12 muffin tins with paper liners or butter and flour the tins; set aside.

2. In a medium bowl, whisk together the flour, sugar, baking powder, and salt; set aside.

3. In a small bowl, whisk the eggs to break them up; whisk in the butter, milk, and vanilla. With a heavy spoon, stir the egg mixture into the dry ingredients just until moistened. Carefully fold in the raspberries with a rubber spatula.

4. Spoon the batter into the prepared tins. Sprinkle the tops with additional sugar, if desired.

5. Bake until the cupcakes are golden and springy when lightly pressed with a fingertip, 15 to 20 minutes. Cool in the tins on a wire rack.

BLUEBERRY CRUMB CAKES

To save time, melt the butter for both the crumbs and the batter at the same time, then divide it in half.

Makes 12 cupcakes

SPICED CRUMBS
½ cup all-purpose flour
⅓ cup sugar
¼ cup (½ stick) unsalted butter, melted
½ teaspoon ground cinnamon

BATTER
1⅓ cups all-purpose flour
½ cup sugar

1 teaspoon baking powder
¼ teaspoon salt
6 tablespoons (¾ stick) unsalted butter, melted and cooled
2 eggs, lightly beaten
¼ cup milk
1 teaspoon pure vanilla extract
1⅓ cups fresh or frozen blueberries

1. Preheat the oven to 375 degrees. Line 12 muffin tins with paper liners or butter and flour the tins; set aside.

2. To make the spiced crumbs, place the butter, flour, sugar and cinnamon in a small bowl and work with your fingers until the mixture forms crumbs; set aside.

3. To make the batter, whisk together the flour, sugar, baking powder, and salt in a medium bowl. Add the melted butter, eggs, milk, and vanilla and stir just until blended. Gently stir in the blueberries.

4. Spoon the batter into the prepared muffin tins. Top with the crumbs, gently pressing them into the batter.

5. Bake until the crumbs and the tops of the cupcakes are golden, the cupcakes are springy when lightly pressed with a fingertip, and the berries burst, 20 to 25 minutes. Cool for 15 minutes in the muffin tins on a wire rack.

LITTLE CINNAMON CRUMB CAKES

Crisp cinnamon-scented crumbs overflow from these quickly prepared cupcakes. For apple or peach crumb cakes, quarter, pare, core, and thinly slice a tart green apple or firm ripe peach. Tuck the fruit slices into the batter before sprinkling with the crumbs.

Makes 12 cupcakes

CRUMBS
½ cup (1 stick) unsalted butter, softened
1 cup all-purpose flour
⅔ cup sugar
2 teaspoons ground cinnamon

BATTER
2¼ cups all-purpose flour

1 cup sugar
1 tablespoon baking powder
¼ teaspoon salt
¾ cup vegetable oil
⅓ cup milk
3 eggs
1 teaspoon pure vanilla extract

1. Preheat the oven to 350 degrees. Line 12 muffin tins with paper liners or butter and flour the tins; set aside.

2. To make the crumbs, place the butter, flour, sugar and cinnamon in a small bowl and work with your fingers until the mixture forms crumbs; set aside.

3. To make the batter, whisk together the flour, sugar, baking powder, and salt in a medium bowl. Add the oil, milk, eggs, and vanilla, and beat vigorously with a heavy spoon just until the batter is blended. Do not overbeat.

4. Spoon the batter into the prepared muffin tins. Scatter the crumbs over the tops, pressing them in gently.

5. Bake until the tops are springy when lightly pressed with a fingertip, the batter is golden, and the crumbs are crisp, about 40 minutes. Cool in the tins on a wire rack for 5 minutes. If the cakes have overflowed a bit, cut them apart with a sharp knife. Carefully unmold the cakes. Serve them warm or at room temperature.

Classic Cupcakes

T he recipes in this chapter use traditional ingredients such as vanilla, brown sugar, and cinnamon. Yellow cupcakes rich in eggs and butter, lemon cupcakes made extra moist with a final dousing of tangy syrup, caramel cupcakes with the flavor of butterscotch—these are the cupcakes of childhood memories.

Maple–walnut cupcakes

Maple Whipped Cream makes a splendid addition to these cupcakes, as does Vanilla Whipped Cream. You can also top the frosted cupcakes with whole walnut halves dipped in caramelized sugar.

Makes 12 cupcakes

¾ cup finely chopped walnuts
1⅓ cups all-purpose flour
1 teaspoon baking powder
½ teaspoon baking soda
¼ teaspoon salt
½ cup (1 stick) unsalted butter, softened

½ cup firmly packed dark brown sugar
½ cup maple syrup
2 eggs
1 teaspoon pure vanilla extract
1 teaspoon maple flavoring

1. Preheat the oven to 350 degrees. While the oven preheats, toast the walnuts in a pie plate (see page 26); set aside to cool.

2. Line 12 muffin tins with paper liners or butter and flour the tins; set aside. In a small bowl, whisk together the flour, baking powder, baking soda, and salt; set aside.

3. In a medium bowl, beat the butter, sugar, and maple syrup with an electric mixer on high speed until they are well blended, light, and fluffy. Lower the mixer speed to medium. Beat in the eggs, then the vanilla extract and maple flavoring.

4. Lower the mixer speed to low. Add the flour mixture to the creamed butter mixture and beat just until blended. Add the chopped nuts.

5. Spoon the batter into the prepared muffin tins.

6. Bake until the tops of the cupcakes are golden and springy when lightly pressed with a fingertip, 20 to 25 minutes. Cool completely in the muffin tins on a wire rack.

GOLD CUPCAKES

Ironically, the tops of these gold-interior cupcakes don't get golden in the oven! To preserve their moist, tender quality, the cupcakes should be removed when they're still springy to the touch. Top with any of the buttercream frostings. If desired, cut off the top third of each cupcake and add 1¹/₂ tablespoons of filling before frosting.

Makes 12 cupcakes

1¼ cups all-purpose flour
1½ teaspoons baking powder
¼ teaspoon salt
6 tablespoons (¾ stick) unsalted
 butter, softened

⅔ cup sugar
3 egg yolks
1 teaspoon pure vanilla extract
½ cup milk

1. Preheat the oven to 350 degrees. Line 12 muffin tins with paper liners or butter and flour the tins; set aside.

2. In a small bowl, whisk together the flour, baking powder, and salt; set aside.

3. In a medium bowl, beat the butter until light with an electric mixer on high speed. Gradually beat in the sugar and continue beating until the mixture is very light and fluffy. Lower the mixer speed to medium. Add the egg yolks, one at a time, beating just until blended, then beat in the vanilla extract. Lower the mixer speed to low. Alternately beat in the flour mixture and the milk, beating just until blended.

4. Spoon the batter into the prepared muffin tins.

5. Bake until the tops of the cupcakes are springy when lightly pressed with a fingertip but not golden in color, 20 to 25 minutes. Cool for 5 minutes in the muffin tins on a wire rack. Transfer the cupcakes to the wire rack and cool completely.

CARAMEL CUPCAKES

With a dense, pound cake–like consistency, these cupcakes, flavored with a simple caramel syrup, go well with coffee, cinnamon, or vanilla icings. I learned the technique for making the syrup from Nick Malgieri's classic book, Nick Malgieri's Perfect Pastry, published by Macmillan in 1989.

Makes 12 cupcakes

CARAMEL SYRUP
½ cup sugar
½ teaspoon fresh lemon juice
¼ cup water

BATTER
1⅓ cups all-purpose flour
1 teaspoon baking powder
⅛ teaspoon salt

½ cup (1 stick) unsalted butter, softened
⅔ cup firmly packed dark brown sugar
1 egg
1 egg yolk
1 teaspoon pure vanilla extract
½ cup sour cream or plain yogurt

1. Preheat the oven to 350 degrees. Line 12 muffin tins with paper liners or butter and flour the tins; set aside.

2. To make the caramel syrup, place the sugar and lemon juice in a small heavy saucepan and stir until the lemon juice is distributed throughout. Place over moderate heat, without stirring, until the sugar begins to melt.

3. When the first sign of smoke appears, begin stirring the melting sugar with a large metal spoon. Continue stirring occasionally, so the sugar will melt and caramelize evenly. When most of the sugar has melted, lower the heat. Continue cooking until the caramel is light amber and frothy; don't be alarmed if it smokes, but don't let it burn, either.

4. Just before the caramel is light amber, bring the water to a boil in a small saucepan. When the caramel is sufficiently cooked, add the water all at once, holding it at arm's length from the caramel and averting your face to avoid getting splattered. When the syrup comes to a full, rolling boil, remove it from the heat and transfer to a heatproof measuring cup. You should have about ½ cup syrup. If not, add a bit of water to make ½ cup. Let the syrup cool while preparing the batter.

5. To make the batter, whisk together the flour, baking powder, and salt in a small bowl; set aside.

6. In a medium bowl, beat the butter until light and fluffy with an electric mixer on high speed; gradually beat in the sugar until very light and fluffy. Lower the mixer speed to medium. Beat in the egg, egg yolk, and vanilla. Lower the mixer speed to low.

7. Beat in the flour mixture alternately with the caramel syrup and the sour cream, just until blended.

8. Spoon the batter into the prepared muffin tins.

9. Bake until the tops of the cupcakes are firm and springy, about 20 minutes. Cool in the muffin tins on a wire rack.

BLACKBERRY JAM CUPCAKES

A lightly spiced batter that gets its sweetness, color, and perfume from seedless blackberry or black raspberry jam. (I've used both varieties; the black raspberry jam gives the cupcakes an intense deep purple color. I've also used all-fruit preserves instead of the sweetened type; this produces a less sweet cupcake.) Spread each cupcake with a white frosting such as Vanilla Buttercream or Snowy White Glaze and crown with one perfect fresh blackberry. Or, spread with additional jam and top with Vanilla Whipped Cream.

Makes 12 cupcakes

1 ⅓ cups all-purpose flour
1 teaspoon baking powder
½ teaspoon baking soda
½ teaspoon ground cinnamon
¼ teaspoon ground nutmeg

¼ teaspoon salt
6 tablespoons (¾ stick) unsalted butter, softened
⅓ cup firmly packed light brown sugar

1 egg
1 teaspoon pure vanilla extract
⅓ cup buttermilk

⅔ cup seedless blackberry or black raspberry jam (see Note)

1. Preheat the oven to 350 degrees. Line 12 muffin tins with paper liners or butter and flour the tins; set aside.

2. In a small bowl, whisk together the flour, baking powder, baking soda, cinnamon, nutmeg, and salt; set aside.

3. In a medium bowl, beat the butter until light and fluffy with an electric mixer on high speed; gradually beat in the sugar until very light and fluffy. Lower the mixer speed to medium. Beat in the egg and the vanilla. Lower the mixer speed to low. Beat in the flour mixture alternately with the buttermilk, just until blended. Beat in the jam until almost but not quite blended into the batter; any lumps of preserves will provide nice bursts of flavor in the cupcakes.

4. Spoon the batter into the prepared muffin tins.

5. Bake until the tops of the cupcakes are springy and the lumps of preserves bubble up, about 20 minutes. Cool in the muffin tins on a wire rack.

Note: If you can't find seedless jam, heat one 12-ounce jar of jam with seeds until melted; strain through a fine sieve into a small bowl; cool completely before measuring and adding to the batter.

GOLDEN VANILLA CUPCAKES

A basic batter that's highly adaptable, whether you stir in chopped nuts and fruit before baking or add a filling to the finished cupcakes. Either way, the intense vanilla flavor imparts a crème brûlée nuance.

Makes 12 cupcakes

1½ cups all-purpose flour
1 teaspoon baking powder
¼ teaspoon salt
½ cup (1 stick) unsalted butter, softened

¾ cup sugar
2 eggs
1 egg yolk
2 teaspoons pure vanilla extract
½ cup milk

1. Preheat the oven to 350 degrees. Line 12 muffin tins with paper liners or butter and flour the tins; set aside.

2. In a small bowl, whisk together the flour, baking powder, and salt; set aside.

3. In a medium bowl, beat the butter until light and fluffy with an electric mixer on high speed. Gradually beat in the sugar until very light and fluffy. Lower the mixer speed to medium. Beat in the eggs, one at a time, the egg yolk, and the vanilla. Lower the mixer speed to low. Beat in the flour mixture alternately with the milk, just until blended.

4. Spoon the batter into the prepared muffin tins.

5. Bake until the tops of the cupcakes are springy when lightly pressed with a fingertip but not quite golden, 20 to 22 minutes. Cool for 15 minutes in the muffin tins on a wire rack.

Rum-raisin cupcakes—I and II

While testing the following recipes, I didn't have the heart to reject either one!

Rum-Raisin Cupcakes I, rich and puddinglike, are too rich to be topped with a buttery frosting. Instead, serve them alongside a tart fruit mixture such as sliced peaches doused with rum or poached dried apricots garnished with toasted almonds.

Rum-Raisin Cupcakes II, cakey and less dense, hold up to a substantial topping such as *Hard-Sauce Frosting*, or a brushing of *Apricot Glaze* followed by a layer of marzipan. They're particularly festive decorated with holly leaves and berries fashioned from marzipan.

RUM-RAISIN CUPCAKES I

Makes 12 cupcakes

⅔ cup raisins
¼ cup rum
⅔ cup all-purpose flour
½ teaspoon baking powder
½ teaspoon baking soda
Large pinch salt
½ cup (1 stick) unsalted butter,
  softened

⅔ cup firmly packed light brown
  sugar
3 egg yolks
1 teaspoon pure vanilla extract
1 teaspoon rum extract (see Note)
⅓ cup sour cream

1. In a small bowl, combine the raisins and the rum. Cover and let stand for at least 4 hours. (The mixture may be left for up to a week; in fact, the raisins will get increasingly plump and fragrant with longer standing.) Just before serving, pulse-chop the raisins and rum in a food processor or blender; reserve.

2. Preheat the oven to 350 degrees. Line 12 muffin tins with paper liners or butter and flour the tins; set aside.

3. In a small bowl, whisk together the flour, baking powder, baking soda, and salt; set aside.

4. In a medium bowl, beat the butter and sugar with an electric mixer on high speed until well blended, light, and fluffy; beat in the egg yolks, then the vanilla and rum extracts. Alternately beat in the sour cream and dry ingredients, just until blended. Beat in the chopped raisin mixture.

5. Spoon the batter into the prepared tins.

6. Bake until the cupcakes are deep golden and springy when lightly pressed with a fingertip, 20 to 25 minutes. Cool in the tins on a wire rack.

Note: Even though most rum extracts are labeled *imitation*, I still like the intensified flavor they provide.

Rum–raisin Cupcakes II

Follow the ingredients and instructions provided for Rum-Raisin Cupcakes I, but reduce the butter to 6 tablespoons (¾ stick), use 2 eggs instead of 3 egg yolks, and increase the flour to ¾ cup.

MOLASSES MARBLE CUPCAKES

Big or small, marble cakes are exciting to the eye and the palate. In this version, yellow and molasses batters swirl together, ready to be topped with Lemon Buttercream.

Makes 12 cupcakes

1 1/4 cups all-purpose flour
1 teaspoon baking powder
1/4 teaspoon salt
1/4 cup molasses
1/2 teaspoon ground cinnamon
1/4 teaspoon ground nutmeg
1/4 teaspoon ground cloves
6 tablespoons (3/4 stick) unsalted butter, softened

2/3 cup sugar
1 egg
1 1/2 teaspoons grated lemon zest
1 teaspoon pure vanilla extract
1/2 cup milk
1/8 teaspoon baking soda

1. Preheat the oven to 350 degrees. Line 12 muffin tins with paper liners or butter and flour the tins; set aside.

2. In a small bowl, whisk together the flour, baking powder, and salt; set aside. In a 1-cup measure, combine the molasses, cinnamon, nutmeg, and cloves; set aside.

3. In a medium bowl, beat the butter until light and fluffy with an electric mixer on high speed; gradually beat in the sugar until very light and fluffy. Lower the mixer speed to medium. Beat in the egg, then the lemon zest and vanilla extract.

4. Lower the mixer speed to low. Alternately beat in the flour mixture and the milk.

5. Stir the baking soda into the molasses mixture. Remove 1 cup of the batter to a small bowl; stir in the molasses mixture.

6. Alternately spoon dollops of yellow and molasses batters into the prepared tins. Using a dinner knife, gently make an X through each mound of batter, to marbleize.

7. Bake until the tops of the cupcakes are soft but springy, 20 to 25 minutes. Cool in the muffin tins on a wire rack.

BUTTERMILK SPICE CUPCAKES

Top these tender cupcakes with Spiced Crumbs, or bake the batter plain and top with Cinnamon Glaze, Lemon Buttercream, or Lemon Curd Cream.

Makes 12 cupcakes

1 ½ cups all-purpose flour
1 teaspoon ground cinnamon
¼ teaspoon ground ginger
⅛ teaspoon ground or grated nutmeg
⅛ teaspoon ground cloves
½ teaspoon baking powder
½ teaspoon baking soda
¼ teaspoon salt
6 tablespoons (¾ stick) unsalted butter, softened

½ cup firmly packed light brown sugar
⅓ cup granulated sugar
2 eggs
1 teaspoon pure vanilla extract
¾ cup buttermilk
Spiced Crumbs (recipe follows) (optional)

1. Preheat the oven to 350 degrees. Line 12 muffin tins with paper liners or butter and flour the tins; set aside.

2. In a small bowl, whisk together the flour, cinnamon, ginger, nutmeg, cloves, baking powder, baking soda, and salt; set aside.

3. In a large mixing bowl, beat the butter and the brown and granulated sugars until light and fluffy with an electric mixer on high speed. Lower the mixer speed to medium. Beat in the eggs, one at a time, then beat in the vanilla. Lower the mixer speed to low. Beat in the flour mixture, alternately with the buttermilk, just until blended.

4. Spoon the batter into the prepared muffin tins. Top with Spiced Crumbs, if desired, pressing them in gently.

5. Bake until the tops of the cupcakes are golden and springy when lightly pressed with a fingertip and the crumbs are golden, 20 to 25 minutes. Cool for 15 minutes in the muffin tins on a wire rack.

SPICED CRUMBS

3 tablespoons unsalted butter, softened
2 tablespoons granulated sugar
2 tablespoons firmly packed light brown sugar

½ cup all-purpose flour
½ teaspoon ground cinnamon
Large pinch ground or grated nutmeg
Large pinch ground cloves

In a small bowl, combine all of the ingredients until the mixture forms coarse crumbs.

GINGERBREAD CUPCAKES

Deeply flavored with molasses, these spicy cupcakes go well with Lemon Buttercream, Cream Cheese Frosting, or Browned Butter Frosting. Because of the traditional addition of boiling water, the eggs are added at the very end, to avoid curdling.

Makes 12 cupcakes

1⅓ cups all-purpose flour
1 teaspoon ground ginger
1 teaspoon ground cinnamon
¼ teaspoon ground cloves
⅛ teaspoon salt
6 tablespoons (¾ stick) unsalted butter, softened

⅓ cup sugar
½ cup unsulfured (mild) molasses
1 teaspoon baking soda
½ cup boiling water
2 eggs

1. Preheat the oven to 350 degrees. Line 12 muffin tins with paper liners or butter and flour the tins; set aside.

2. In a small bowl, whisk together the flour, ginger, cinnamon, cloves, and salt; set aside.

3. In a medium bowl, beat the butter until light and fluffy with an electric mixer on high speed; gradually beat in the sugar until the mixture is very light and fluffy, then beat in the molasses. Lower the mixer speed to medium.

4. Stir the baking soda into the boiling water; beat into the butter mixture. Lower the mixer speed to low. Sift the flour mixture, a third at a time, over the butter mixture and beat in, just until blended. Beat in the eggs.

5. Pour the batter into the prepared muffin tins. (This is most easily done by transferring the batter to a pitcher with a spout.)

6. Bake until the tops of the cupcakes are firm and springy, about 20 minutes. Cool in the muffin tins on a wire rack.

POPPY SEED CUPCAKES

Subtly flavored with orange and lemon, these speckled cupcakes can be topped with Lemon Glaze and sprinkled with additional poppy seeds before the glaze sets.

Makes 12 cupcakes

2 tablespoons poppy seeds
2 tablespoons milk
1 ⅓ cups all-purpose flour
½ teaspoon baking powder
½ teaspoon baking soda
¼ teaspoon salt
½ cup (1 stick) unsalted butter, softened

¾ cup sugar
2 eggs
1 teaspoon grated orange zest
1 teaspoon grated lemon zest
½ teaspoon pure vanilla extract
⅓ cup fresh orange juice
2 tablespoons fresh lemon juice

1. In a small saucepan, combine the poppy seeds and the milk. Bring to a simmer over moderate heat; remove from the heat and let stand for 30 minutes.

2. Meanwhile, preheat the oven to 350 degrees. Line 12 muffin tins with paper liners or butter and flour the tins; set aside.

3. In a small bowl, whisk together the flour, baking powder, baking soda, and salt; set aside.

4. In a medium bowl, beat the butter until light and fluffy with an electric mixer on high speed; gradually beat in the sugar until very light and fluffy. Lower the mixer speed to medium. Beat in the eggs, one at a time, then beat in the poppy-seed mixture, orange and lemon zests, and vanilla. Lower the mixer speed to low. Beat in the flour mixture alternately with the orange and lemon juices, just until blended.

5. Spoon the batter into the prepared muffin tins.

6. Bake until the tops of the cupcakes are golden and springy when lightly pressed with a fingertip, about 20 minutes. Cool for 15 minutes in the muffin tins on a wire rack.

LEMONY BUTTERMILK CUPCAKES

A hint of lemon zest enhances the tangy buttermilk flavor. Top with Lemon Buttercream or Lemon Glaze. Serve with berries.

Makes 12 cupcakes

1 ½ cups all-purpose flour
1 teaspoon baking powder
½ teaspoon baking soda
¼ teaspoon salt
½ cup buttermilk
Grated zest of 1 lemon (about
  2 teaspoons)

1 teaspoon pure vanilla extract
½ cup (1 stick) unsalted butter,
  softened
¾ cup sugar
1 egg
1 egg yolk

1. Preheat the oven to 350 degrees. Line 12 muffin tins with paper liners or butter and flour the tins; set aside.

2. In a small bowl, whisk together the flour, baking powder, baking soda, and salt; set aside. In a second small bowl, combine the buttermilk, lemon zest, and vanilla; set aside.

3. In a medium bowl, beat the butter until light and fluffy with an electric mixer on high speed. Gradually beat in the sugar and continue beating until the mixture is very light and fluffy. Lower the mixer speed to medium. Beat in the egg, then the egg yolk. Lower the mixer speed to low. Beat in the flour mixture alternately with the buttermilk mixture, just until blended.

4. Spoon the batter into the prepared muffin tins.

5. Bake until the tops of the cupcakes are golden and springy when lightly pressed with a fingertip, 20 to 22 minutes. Cool for 15 minutes in the muffin tins on a wire rack.

Extra-moist lemon cupcakes

These cupcakes, with their tangy syrup topping, are moist enough to serve with just a dusting of confectioners' sugar. Tried-and-true citrus lovers will appreciate the addition of Lemon Curd as a filling or Lemon Buttercream on top.

Makes 12 cupcakes

BATTER
1⅓ cups all-purpose flour
½ teaspoon baking soda
½ teaspoon baking powder
⅛ teaspoon salt
6 tablespoons (¾ stick) unsalted butter, softened
⅔ cup sugar
2 eggs

1 tablespoon grated lemon zest
2 tablespoons fresh lemon juice
¼ teaspoon pure lemon extract
½ cup plain yogurt

LEMON SYRUP
3 tablespoons fresh lemon juice
3 tablespoons sugar

1. Preheat the oven to 350 degrees. Line 12 muffin tins with paper liners or butter and flour the tins; set aside.

2. To make the batter, whisk together the flour, baking soda, baking powder, and salt in a small bowl; set aside.

3. In a medium bowl, beat the butter until light and fluffy with an electric mixer on high speed. Gradually beat in the sugar, and continue beating until the mixture is very light and fluffy. Lower the mixer speed to medium. Beat in the eggs, one at a time, beating just until blended, then beat in the lemon zest and juice and the lemon extract. Lower the mixer speed to low. Alternately beat in the flour mixture and the yogurt, beating just until blended.

4. Spoon the batter into the prepared muffin tins.

5. Bake until the tops of the cupcakes are springy when lightly pressed with a fingertip, but not golden, about 20 minutes. Cool for 15 minutes in the muffin tins on a wire rack.

6. To make the syrup, stir the lemon juice and sugar together in a small cup. Gently remove the paper liners from the cupcakes; return the cupcakes to the tins. Spoon the syrup over the still-warm cupcakes, letting it flow over the sides and into the bottom of the tins. Cool completely on the wire rack. Handle the cupcakes very gently, since they will be very tender and sticky.

CHERRY CHIP CUPCAKES

Maraschino cherry juice gives the batter a delicate pink color, an attractive background for the chips and cherry pieces. Top with any chocolate or vanilla frosting. For a garnish, what could be better than a big maraschino cherry?

Makes 12 cupcakes

1⅓ cups all-purpose flour
1 teaspoon baking powder
⅛ teaspoon salt
¼ cup milk
¼ cup syrup from maraschino
  cherries
1 teaspoon pure vanilla extract
¼ teaspoon pure almond extract

½ cup (1 stick) unsalted butter,
  softened
⅔ cup sugar
2 eggs
½ cup miniature semisweet chocolate
  pieces
¼ cup finely chopped drained
  maraschino cherries (about 14)

1. Preheat the oven to 350 degrees. Line 12 muffin tins with paper liners or butter and flour the tins; set aside.

2. In a small bowl, whisk together the flour, baking powder, and salt; set aside. In a cup, combine the milk, maraschino cherry syrup, and vanilla and almond extracts; the mixture will curdle—don't worry! Set aside.

3. In a medium bowl, beat the butter until light and fluffy with an electric mixer on high speed. Gradually beat in the sugar and continue beating until the mixture is very light and fluffy. Lower the mixer speed to medium. Add the eggs, one at a time, beating just until blended. Lower the mixer speed to low. Alternately beat in the flour mixture and the milk mixture, beating just until blended. Beat in the chocolate chips and cherries.

4. Spoon the batter into the prepared muffin tins.

5. Bake until the tops of the cupcakes are golden and springy when lightly pressed with a fingertip, 20 to 25 minutes. Cool for 15 minutes in the muffin tins on a wire rack.

Honey cupcakes

These cupcakes, kissed with a medley of spices, call for golden raisins, but you can substitute other dried fruits, such as dark raisins, currants, or dried cherries. Or, use some of each! The honey makes these good keepers; in fact, they improve with a day's aging.

Makes 12 cupcakes

¾ cup honey
½ cup extra-strength coffee
¼ cup firmly packed light brown
  sugar
⅓ cup vegetable oil
¼ cup fresh orange juice
1⅓ cups all-purpose flour
½ teaspoon baking powder
½ teaspoon baking soda

1 teaspoon ground cinnamon
½ teaspoon ground allspice
½ teaspoon ground ginger
⅛ teaspoon ground cloves
⅛ teaspoon ground or grated
  nutmeg
¼ teaspoon salt
2 eggs
½ cup golden raisins

1. Preheat the oven to 350 degrees. Line 12 muffin tins with paper liners or butter and flour the tins; set aside.

2. In a small saucepan, combine the honey, coffee, brown sugar, oil, and orange juice. Place over moderate heat and cook, stirring often, until the mixture is warm and the brown sugar has dissolved. Remove from the heat; set aside to cool to lukewarm.

3. Meanwhile, in a small bowl, whisk together the flour, baking powder, baking soda, cinnamon, allspice, ginger, cloves, nutmeg, and salt; set aside.

4. In a medium bowl, whisk the eggs to break them up. Whisk in half of the warm honey mixture until the mixture is smooth, then whisk in the remainder. Whisk in the sifted dry ingredients just until blended, then whisk in the raisins.

5. Pour the batter into the prepared muffin tins, distributing the raisins evenly. (Pouring is easier if you transfer the batter to a pitcher.) The tins will look dangerously full, but don't worry—the cupcakes will bake evenly and won't overflow!

6. Bake until the cupcakes are springy when lightly pressed with a fingertip, 20 to 25 minutes. Cool in the tins on a wire rack.

HOT-MILK
SPONGE CAKES

These light cupcakes are nice on their own, served with drifts of softly whipped cream and fresh fruit. They're also simple enough to figure in more elaborate preparations such as "Truffles," "Cuppuccinos," or Little Boston Cream Pies. Like all sponge cakes, they're extra tender when made with cake flour.

Makes 12 cupcakes

1 cup cake flour (not self-rising)	¾ cup sugar
1 teaspoon baking powder	1 teaspoon pure vanilla extract
Large pinch salt	½ cup milk
2 eggs	¼ cup (½ stick) unsalted butter

1. Preheat the oven to 350 degrees. Line 12 muffin tins with paper liners or butter and flour the tins; set aside.

2. Sift together the flour, baking powder, and salt onto a sheet of waxed paper; set aside.

3. In a medium bowl, beat the eggs with an electric mixer on high speed until they are very light, about 5 minutes. Slowly add the sugar in a fine stream and continue beating until the mixture is very thick and light, about 3 minutes longer. Beat in the vanilla.

4. While the eggs are being beaten, heat the milk and the butter over moderately low heat. When the eggs are ready, bring the milk-and-butter mixture just to a boil. Don't worry if the milk curdles.

5. Lower the mixer speed to low; beat in the sifted dry ingredients, then slowly beat in the boiling milk mixture. The batter will be thin but beautifully smooth. Transfer the batter, in batches, to a 2-cup measure with a spout. Immediately pour the batter into the prepared tins. The tins will be full!

6. Bake until the cupcakes are light golden and springy when lightly pressed with a fingertip, 20 to 23 minutes. Cool in the tins on a wire rack for about 5 minutes, then carefully transfer the cupcakes to the wire rack to cool completely. Store the cupcakes in a tightly closed container if you won't be serving them in a short time, to prevent them from drying out.

Chocolate Cupcakes

For some people, it isn't dessert if it isn't chocolate. (I certainly fall into this category!) The recipes included here run the gamut from tender cupcakes based on cocoa powder to dense, intense treats made to savor oh-so-slowly. Top them with a rich chocolate frosting from chapter 9, or one of a contrasting color and flavor.

ESPRESSO–CHOCOLATE CHIP CUPCAKES

Top these with Espresso Glaze and a whole coffee bean dipped in chocolate. The 3 tablespoons of espresso powder produces an intense bittersweet flavor appreciated by confirmed coffee lovers; 2 tablespoons provides a more subtle result.

Makes 12 cupcakes

1⅓ cups all-purpose flour
½ teaspoon baking powder
½ teaspoon baking soda
¼ teaspoon salt
6 tablespoons (¾ stick) unsalted butter, softened
⅓ cup granulated sugar
⅓ cup firmly packed light brown sugar

1 egg
2 to 3 tablespoons instant espresso powder
1 teaspoon pure vanilla extract
½ cup milk
½ cup finely chopped walnuts
1 bar (3 ounces) bittersweet chocolate, chopped/ground very fine (see Note)

1. Preheat the oven to 350 degrees. Line 12 muffin tins with paper liners or butter and flour the tins; set aside.

2. In a small bowl, whisk together the flour, baking powder, baking soda, and salt; set aside.

3. In a medium bowl, beat the butter until light and fluffy with an electric mixer on high speed. Gradually beat in the granulated and brown sugars. Lower the mixer speed to medium. Beat in the egg, espresso powder, and vanilla. Lower the mixer speed to low. Alternately beat in the flour mixture and the milk, just until blended. Fold in the chopped walnuts and chocolate.

4. Spoon the batter into the prepared muffin tins.

5. Bake until the tops of the cupcakes are springy when lightly pressed with a fingertip, about 20 minutes. Cool for 5 minutes in the muffin tins on a wire rack.

Note: To chop/grind the chocolate very fine, break it into pieces and pulse-chop in a food processor. Some of the chocolate will be pulverized, the rest will remain in very small pieces.

MARBLED CHOCOLATE-ORANGE CUPCAKES

Top these with Orange Glaze, if desired, or with a chocolate buttercream.

Makes 12 cupcakes

CHOCOLATE MARBLE MIXTURE
1/4 cup unsweetened cocoa powder
3 tablespoons sugar
1/8 teaspoon baking soda
2 tablespoons water
1 teaspoon pure vanilla extract

BATTER
1 1/4 cups all-purpose flour
1/2 teaspoon baking powder
1/2 teaspoon baking soda

1/4 teaspoon salt
1/2 cup (1 stick) unsalted butter, softened
3/4 cup sugar
2 eggs
1/2 cup sour cream or plain yogurt
1/2 cup fresh orange juice (from about 1 orange)
Grated zest of 1 orange (about 1 tablespoon)

1. Preheat the oven to 350 degrees. Line 12 muffin tins with paper liners or butter and flour the tins; set aside.

2. To make the chocolate marble mixture, whisk together the cocoa, 3 tablespoons sugar, and baking soda in a small bowl. Beat in the water and vanilla until smooth; set aside.

3. To make the batter, whisk together the flour, baking powder, baking soda, and salt in a small bowl; set aside.

4. In a medium bowl, beat the butter until light and fluffy with an electric mixer on high speed; gradually beat in the ¾ cup sugar and continue beating until the mixture is very light and fluffy. Lower the mixer speed to medium. Beat in the eggs, one at a time, then beat in the sour cream. Lower the mixer speed to low. Beat in the flour mixture alternately with the orange juice, just until blended.

5. Remove about 1 cup of the batter; stir into the chocolate marble mixture. Stir the orange zest into the remaining batter.

6. Spoon the orange batter into the prepared muffin tins; top with the chocolate batter. Gently swirl the batter in the tins once or twice, using a knife or a spoon handle.

7. Bake until the tops of the cupcakes are golden and springy when lightly pressed with a fingertip, about 20 minutes. Cool for 15 minutes in the muffin tins on a wire rack.

Tender chocolate cupcakes

These cupcakes are light and moist, not exceptionally fudgy. Fill them with Vanilla Whipped Cream, then top with Chocolate Satin Glaze and a final flourish of Squiggle Frosting, to simulate those famous cupcakes beloved from childhood.

Makes 12 cupcakes

1 cup all-purpose flour
½ teaspoon baking powder
½ teaspoon baking soda
¼ teaspoon salt
6 tablespoons (¾ stick) unsalted butter, softened

1 cup sugar
2 eggs
2 squares (1 ounce each) unsweetened chocolate, melted and cooled
1 teaspoon pure vanilla extract
½ cup milk

1. Preheat the oven to 350 degrees. Line 12 muffin tins with paper liners or butter and flour the tins; set aside.

2. In a small bowl, whisk together the flour, baking powder, baking soda, and salt; set aside.

3. In a medium bowl, beat the butter until light and fluffy with an electric mixer on high speed. Gradually add the sugar, beating after each addition, and continue beating until the mixture is very light and fluffy. Lower the mixer speed to medium. Beat in the eggs, one at a time, then beat in the melted chocolate and vanilla. Lower the mixer speed to low. Alternately beat in the flour mixture and the milk, just until blended.

4. Spoon the batter into the prepared muffin tins.

5. Bake until the tops of the cupcakes are springy when lightly pressed with a fingertip, 15 to 20 minutes. Cool for 15 minutes in the muffin tins on a wire rack.

CHOCOLATE–WALNUT CUPCAKES

These cupcakes, scented with bourbon, have a "grown-up" taste and texture. For an elegant presentation, drizzle them with Microwave Fudge Sauce and serve them on a pool of bourbon-flavored crème anglaise. Or, brush the baked cupcakes with Apricot Glaze and top with Chocolate Satin Glaze, for miniature Sacher tortes.

Makes 12 cupcakes

2 squares (1 ounce each) unsweetened chocolate
½ cup brewed coffee
⅓ cup granulated sugar
⅓ cup walnuts
1¼ cups all-purpose flour
½ teaspoon baking powder

½ teaspoon baking soda
¼ teaspoon salt
6 tablespoons (¾ stick) unsalted
  butter, softened
⅔ cup firmly packed light brown
  sugar
2 eggs

1 tablespoon bourbon, rum, or walnut liqueur

1 teaspoon pure vanilla extract

1. Preheat the oven to 350 degrees. Line 12 muffin tins with paper liners or butter and flour the tins; set aside.

2. In a small saucepan over low heat, melt the chocolate in the coffee. Remove from the heat and let stand while preparing the rest of the batter.

3. In the work bowl of a food processor, process the granulated sugar and the walnuts until the walnuts are ground; set aside. In a small bowl, whisk together the flour, baking powder, baking soda, and salt; set aside.

4. In a large mixing bowl, beat the butter and the brown sugar until light and fluffy with an electric mixer on high speed. Add the walnut sugar gradually, beating after each addition, and continue beating until the mixture is very light and fluffy. Lower the mixer speed to medium. Beat in the eggs, one at a time, then beat in the melted chocolate, bourbon, and vanilla. Lower the mixer speed to low. Beat in the flour mixture, just until blended.

5. Spoon the batter into the prepared muffin tins.

6. Bake until the top surfaces spring back when lightly pressed with a fingertip but the centers are still a bit soft, about 15 minutes.

7. Cool in the muffin tins on a wire rack for about 10 minutes. Carefully transfer to the wire rack to cool completely.

DEVIL'S FOOD CUPCAKES

As legend has it, these acquired their devilish association from the red tinge the baking soda gives them. Despite their name, they're heavenly light, moist, and tender.

Makes 12 cupcakes

2 squares (1 ounce each) unsweetened chocolate
1 cup all-purpose flour
½ teaspoon baking soda
⅛ teaspoon salt
6 tablespoons (¾ stick) unsalted
butter, softened

⅔ cup firmly packed light brown
sugar
1 egg
1 teaspoon pure vanilla extract
½ cup milk

1. Preheat the oven to 350 degrees. Line 12 muffin tins with paper liners or butter and flour the tins; set aside.

2. Melt the chocolate in a small heavy saucepan over very low heat or in the microwave (see page 22).

3. In a small bowl, whisk together the flour, baking soda, and salt; set aside.

4. In a medium bowl, beat the butter until light and fluffy with an electric mixer on high speed; gradually beat in the sugar until very light and fluffy. Lower the mixer speed to medium. Beat in the egg, the still-warm chocolate, and the vanilla. Lower the mixer speed to low. Beat in the flour mixture alternately with the milk, just until blended.

5. Spoon the batter into the prepared muffin tins.

6. Bake until the tops of the cupcakes are firm and springy, about 20 minutes. Cool in the muffin tins on a wire rack.

MOCHA CUPCAKES

For an elegant presentation, split these Kahlúa-spiked cupcakes in half, sprinkle the cut surfaces with Kahlúa, spread them with Mocha Buttercream, then top with Coffee Glaze.

Makes 12 cupcakes

1⅓ cups all-purpose flour
½ teaspoon baking powder
½ teaspoon baking soda
¼ teaspoon salt
½ cup (1 stick) unsalted butter, softened
1 cup firmly packed dark and/or light brown sugar

1 egg
1 egg yolk
½ cup unsweetened cocoa powder
1 teaspoon pure vanilla extract
⅓ cup milk
⅓ cup cold strong brewed coffee
2 tablespoons Kahlúa or other coffee liqueur

1. Preheat the oven to 350 degrees. Line 12 muffin tins with paper liners or butter and flour the tins; set aside.

2. In a small bowl, whisk together the flour, baking powder, baking soda, and salt; set aside.

3. In a medium bowl, beat the butter until light and fluffy with an electric mixer on high speed. Gradually add the sugar, beating after each addition, and continue beating until the mixture is very light and fluffy. Lower the mixer speed to medium. Add the egg and egg yolk, then beat in the cocoa powder and vanilla.

4. Lower the mixer speed to low. Alternately beat in the sifted dry ingredients and the milk, coffee, and Kahlúa, beginning and ending with the dry ingredients.

5. Spoon the batter into the prepared muffin tins.

6. Bake until the cupcakes spring back when lightly pressed with a fingertip, about 20 minutes. Cool the cupcakes in the muffin tins on a wire rack.

WINTERTIME SACHER CUPCAKES

Fresh cranberry pieces provide bursts of tartness in these cupcakes, which are topped with cranberry sauce, then enrobed in a deep chocolate glaze, producing a European-style texture and flavor—not too sweet, and dense rather than spongy. The glaze sets to a lustrous sheen but remains soft on the inside.

Makes 12 cupcakes

CUPCAKES

2 bars (3 ounces each) semisweet chocolate, chopped, or 1 cup (6 ounces) semisweet chocolate pieces

¾ cup (1½ sticks) unsalted butter, softened

½ cup sugar

4 eggs, separated

¾ cup all-purpose flour, sifted if lumpy

¾ cup fresh or frozen raw cranberries, chopped fine (see Note)

⅛ teaspoon salt

CRANBERRY TOPPING (OR USE 2 TABLESPOONS CRANBERRY WHIP, PAGE 202)

3 tablespoons whole-berry cranberry sauce

1 teaspoon cranberry liqueur or rum

CHOCOLATE GLAZE
8 ounces semisweet chocolate, chopped
⅓ cup sugar

⅓ cup water
¼ cup (½ stick) unsalted butter

12 cranberries rolled in granulated sugar, for decorating the cupcakes

1. To make the cupcakes, preheat the oven to 350 degrees. Line 12 muffin tins with paper liners or butter and flour the tins; set aside.

2. Melt the chocolate in the top of a double boiler over, not in, simmering water or microwave the chocolate (see page 22). Remove from the heat; let cool slightly.

3. In a medium bowl, beat the butter until light and fluffy with an electric mixer on high speed. Gradually beat in the sugar and continue beating until the mixture is very light and fluffy. Lower the mixer speed to medium. Add the egg yolks, half at a time, beating well after each addition. Lower the mixer speed to low; beat in the melted chocolate until blended. Beat in the flour just until it is absorbed, then fold in the chopped cranberries.

4. In a separate bowl with clean beaters, beat the egg whites and salt until soft peaks form. Stir about one fourth of the egg whites into the chocolate mixture. Fold in the remainder, about one fourth at a time.

5. Quickly pour the batter into the prepared tins, gently smoothing the tops.

6. Bake until the tops are firm and spring back when lightly pressed with a fingertip, 15 to 20 minutes. Let the cupcakes cool in the tins on a wire rack for 10 minutes. Carefully invert the cakes onto the rack, then turn them right side up. Let them cool completely on the rack. The cupcakes will shrink. If you used paper liners, carefully peel them away from the cupcakes. Place the cupcakes back on the wire rack.

7. To make the cranberry topping, combine the cranberry sauce and liqueur in a small saucepan; bring to a boil over moderate heat. Spoon the hot sauce over the tops of the cupcakes, carefully spreading to make an even layer and crushing any large pieces of cranberry. Alternatively, spread about ½ teaspoon of Cranberry Whip on top of each cupcake.

8. To make the chocolate glaze, place the chocolate, sugar, and water in the top of a double boiler. Place over, not in, simmering water. Heat, stirring occasionally, until the chocolate melts and the mixture is smooth. Remove from the hot water. Add the butter and stir until it melts. Let the glaze stand at room temperature, stirring occasionally, for about 20 minutes, or until it starts to thicken.

9. Place the cupcakes on the wire rack over a large piece of waxed paper or aluminum foil. Carefully spread the glaze over the tops of the cupcakes with a butter knife so some runs over the sides. Scrape off whatever glaze runs onto the paper and reuse it to glaze the sides of the cupcakes. Let the cupcakes stand for at least an hour, until the outside of the glaze sets. If the glaze is still soft, place the cupcakes in the refrigerator. Decorate the cupcakes with sugar-frosted cranberries and serve with rum-flavored whipped cream, if desired.

Note: The cranberries are easy to chop in the food processor; for best results, process with on-off pulses. If you have raw cranberries in the freezer, chop them while they are still frozen.

CHOCOLATE VALENCIA CUPCAKES

A touch of orange—both in the batter and in the frosting—flavors these deep-chocolate cupcakes. If desired, orange liqueur can be substituted for part of the juice in the frosting.

Makes 12 cupcakes

CUPCAKES
1¼ cups all-purpose flour
½ teaspoon baking powder
½ teaspoon baking soda
¼ teaspoon salt
6 tablespoons (¾ stick) unsalted butter, softened
¾ cup sugar
2 eggs
2 squares (1 ounce each) unsweetened chocolate, melted and cooled
1 tablespoon grated orange zest
1 teaspoon pure vanilla extract
½ cup fresh orange juice

CHOCOLATE-ORANGE FROSTING
2 cups unsifted confectioners' sugar
⅔ cup unsweetened cocoa
Large pinch salt
¼ cup fresh orange juice
2 teaspoons grated orange zest
½ teaspoon pure vanilla extract
¼ cup (½ stick) unsalted butter, softened

1 tablespoon orange liqueur, for sprinkling on the cupcakes (optional)

1. To make the cupcakes, preheat the oven to 350 degrees. Line 12 muffin tins with paper liners or butter and flour the tins; set aside.

2. In a small bowl, whisk together the flour, baking powder, baking soda, and salt; set aside.

3. In a medium bowl, beat the butter until light and fluffy with an electric mixer on high speed. Gradually beat in the sugar, beating well after each addition, and continue beating until the mixture is very light and fluffy. Lower the mixer speed to medium. Beat in the eggs, one at a time, then beat in the melted chocolate, orange zest, and vanilla. Lower the mixer speed to low. Alternately beat in the flour mixture and the orange juice, just until blended.

4. Spoon the batter into the prepared muffin tins.

5. Bake until the tops of the cupcakes are springy when lightly pressed with a fingertip, 15 to 20 minutes. Cool for 15 minutes in the muffin tins on a wire rack. Transfer to the wire rack. Cool completely.

6. To make the frosting, combine the sugar, cocoa, and salt in a small bowl, until blended. Add the orange juice and zest and vanilla; beat until smooth with a hand mixer or a large heavy spoon. Beat in the butter. The frosting should be spreadable. If not, refrigerate it for about 15 minutes.

7. Sprinkle the liqueur over the tops of the cupcakes, if desired. Frost.

FUDGE BROWNIE CUPCAKES

Shiny and crackled on top, with a soft interior, these straddle the dividing line between cakey brownies and fudgy cupcakes. Serve them warm, dusted with confectioners' sugar and accompanied by ice cream. Or, let them cool and top them with Chocolate Satin Glaze, Cocoa Frosting, or Vanilla Whipped Cream piped through a pastry bag fitted with a star tip. If desired, substitute ⅓ cup chocolate-covered raisins for the nuts.

Makes 12 cupcakes

3 squares (1 ounce each) unsweetened chocolate
½ cup (1 stick) unsalted butter
⅔ cup all-purpose flour
¼ teaspoon baking powder
Large pinch salt

2 eggs, lightly beaten
1 cup plus 2 tablespoons sugar
1½ teaspoons pure vanilla extract
¼ cup milk
⅓ cup chopped pecans or walnuts

1. Preheat the oven to 325 degrees. Line 12 muffin tins with paper liners or butter and flour the tins; set aside.

2. In a small saucepan over low heat, melt the chocolate and butter together, stirring often. Remove from the heat. Let cool slightly.

3. In a small bowl, whisk together the flour, baking powder, and salt; set aside.

4. In a medium bowl, beat the eggs until frothy with an electric mixer on high speed. Slowly beat in the sugar and continue beating until the mixture is light and thick. Lower the mixer speed to low. Beat in the chocolate mixture, then the vanilla extract.

5. Alternately beat in the flour mixture and the milk, beginning and ending with the flour mixture. Beat in the nuts. Transfer the batter to a 2-cup glass measure or a small pitcher with a spout.

6. Pour the batter into the prepared muffin tins.

7. Bake until the cupcakes are shiny and crackled on top, firm around the edge but still very soft in the middle, 25 to 30 minutes.

8. Cool in the muffin tins on a wire rack for about 10 minutes. Gently pry the cupcakes from the tins with a small knife and carefully transfer them to the wire rack to cool completely.

FUDGY MINT CUPCAKES

These dense treats are a cross between brownies and cupcakes, with crisp, almost cookielike tops. A lustrous mint-chocolate glaze intensifies the flavor combination. For a striking garnish, top with streaks of Snowy-White Glaze tinted mint green.

Makes 12 cupcakes

BATTER
1 package (10 ounces) semisweet
  mint-chocolate pieces
½ cup (1 stick) unsalted butter
1¼ cups all-purpose flour
½ teaspoon baking powder
½ teaspoon baking soda
⅛ teaspoon salt
2 eggs

¾ cup sugar
⅓ cup sour cream
½ teaspoon pure vanilla extract

GLAZE
⅓ cup heavy or whipping cream
1 tablespoon unsalted butter
1 tablespoon light corn syrup

1. Preheat the oven to 350 degrees. Line 12 muffin tins with paper liners or butter and flour the tins; set aside.

2. To make the batter, melt 1 cup of the chips and the butter in a small heavy saucepan over low heat, stirring often to prevent burning. Remove from the heat; set aside while preparing the rest of the batter.

3. In a small bowl, whisk together the flour, baking powder, baking soda, and salt; set aside.

4. In a medium bowl, beat the eggs with an electric mixer on high speed for about 1 minute. Gradually beat in the sugar until the mixture is light. Lower the mixer speed to medium. Beat in the melted chocolate mixture, sour cream, and vanilla. Lower the mixer speed to low.

5. Beat in the flour mixture, one third at a time, just until blended into a batter.

6. Spoon the batter into the prepared muffin tins.

7. Bake until the tops of the cupcakes are crackled and shiny but still quite soft when lightly pressed with a fingertip, about 20 minutes. Cool completely in the muffin tins on a wire rack.

8. To make the glaze, bring the cream to a simmer in a small heavy saucepan over moderate heat. Add the remaining mint-chocolate chips (about $\frac{1}{2}$ cup), the butter, and the corn syrup, shaking the pan to immerse the chips and the butter completely in the hot cream. Let stand 1 minute, then beat with a spoon until smooth.

9. Since the glaze overflows a bit over the tops of the cupcakes, if desired, remove the paper liners from the cupcakes. Place the cupcakes on the wire rack over a sheet of aluminum foil. With a spoon or your finger, gently make a center depression in the top of each cupcake (this will hold some of the glaze). Spoon the glaze over the cupcakes. Let stand until it sets.

Fruit and Nut Cupcakes

Fruit and nuts celebrate the bounty of the earth, whether featured alone or together. This chapter includes cupcakes using both fresh and dried fruits, and a variety of nuts. Both add flavor, texture, and color to cupcake batters. Chocolate frostings bring out the best in both fruit and nut cupcakes, but other toppings work equally well.

PRUNE-WALNUT CUPCAKES

These cupcakes, a cross between fruitcakes and sponge cakes, go very well with Cinnamon or Lemon Buttercream, as well as with all of the chocolate-flavored icings.

Makes 12 cupcakes

⅔ cup walnuts
1 cup all-purpose flour
1 teaspoon ground cinnamon
1 teaspoon baking powder
¼ teaspoon salt
¾ cup finely chopped pitted prunes
  (about 18)

¾ cup sugar
½ cup (1 stick) unsalted butter,
  softened
2 eggs
2 egg yolks
2 teaspoons pure vanilla extract

1. Preheat the oven to 350 degrees. While the oven preheats, toast the walnuts in a pie plate (see page 26). Allow to cool.

2. Meanwhile, line 12 muffin tins with paper liners or butter and flour the tins; set aside.

In a small bowl, whisk together the flour, cinnamon, baking powder, and salt; toss with the chopped prunes until the prunes are evenly dusted with the flour. Set aside.

3. Place the sugar and cooled nuts in the work bowl of a food processor; process until the nuts are finely ground.

4. In a medium bowl, beat the butter with an electric mixer on high speed until light and fluffy; gradually beat in the walnut-sugar mixture, beating after each addition, and continue beating until the mixture is very light and fluffy. Lower the mixer speed to medium. Beat in the eggs and the egg yolks, one at a time, then the vanilla. Lower the mixer speed to low. Beat in the flour-and-prune mixture, just until blended.

5. Spoon the batter into the prepared muffin tins.

6. Bake until the tops of the cupcakes are springy and cracked, 20 to 25 minutes. (They'll give a "spongy" sound when pressed!) Cool in the muffin tins on a wire rack.

BANANA CRUNCH CUPCAKES

Filled __and__ topped with cinnamon-walnut crunch, these cupcakes are the perfect way to use up that banana that's too ripe to eat.

Makes 12 cupcakes

WALNUT CRUNCH
¾ cup finely chopped walnuts,
  toasted if desired (see page 26)
¼ cup sugar
1½ teaspoons ground cinnamon

BATTER
1 cup all-purpose flour
1½ teaspoons baking powder

⅛ teaspoon salt
½ cup (1 stick) unsalted butter,
  softened
½ cup sugar
1 egg
½ cup sour cream or plain yogurt
½ cup mashed ripe banana (1 large
  banana)
1½ teaspoons pure vanilla extract

1. Preheat the oven to 350 degrees. Line 12 muffin tins with paper liners or butter and flour the tins; set aside.

2. To make the walnut crunch, combine the walnuts, sugar, and cinnamon in a small bowl; set aside.

3. To make the batter, whisk together the flour, baking powder, and salt in a small bowl; set aside.

4. In a medium bowl, beat the butter until light and fluffy with an electric mixer on high speed; gradually beat in the sugar, beating after each addition, and continue beating until the mixture is very light and fluffy. Lower the mixer speed to medium. Beat in the egg, then beat in the sour cream, mashed banana, and vanilla. Lower the mixer speed to low. Beat in the flour mixture, just until blended.

5. Spoon about half of the batter into the prepared muffin tins. Sprinkle about half of the walnut crunch mixture over the batter. Top with the remaining batter, smoothing the tops, then top with the remaining walnut crunch, pressing it in gently to adhere.

6. Bake until the tops of the cupcakes are golden and springy when lightly pressed with a fingertip and the walnuts are toasted, 25 to 28 minutes. Cool for 15 minutes in the muffin tins on a wire rack.

ZUCCHINI CUPCAKES

Little flecks of green permeate the quickly prepared batter. Cream Cheese Frosting (perhaps tinted light green!) is a nice topping.

Makes 12 cupcakes

1 ⅓ cups all-purpose flour
1 teaspoon baking soda
½ teaspoon baking powder
½ teaspoon ground cinnamon
¼ teaspoon salt

2 eggs
1 cup sugar
¾ cup vegetable oil
1 teaspoon pure vanilla extract
1 cup grated zucchini (including peel)

1. Preheat the oven to 350 degrees. Line 12 muffin tins with paper liners or butter and flour the tins; set aside.

2. In a small bowl, whisk together the flour, baking soda, baking powder, cinnamon, and salt; set aside.

3. In a medium bowl with an electric mixer on high speed, beat the eggs, sugar, oil, and vanilla until thick and well blended. Beat in the zucchini, then the dry ingredients, just until blended.

4. Spoon the batter into the prepared muffin tins.

5. Bake until the cupcakes are golden brown and the tops are springy when lightly pressed with a fingertip, about 20 minutes. Cool in the tins on a wire rack for 5 minutes. Carefully transfer the cupcakes to the wire rack. Cool completely.

AUTUMN APPLESAUCE CUPCAKES

Studded with chopped dates, raisins, and walnuts, these hearty cupcakes go well with orange-flavored Cream Cheese Frosting.

Makes 12 cupcakes

1⅓ cups all-purpose flour
1 teaspoon ground cinnamon
½ teaspoon ground ginger
1 teaspoon baking powder
½ teaspoon baking soda
¼ teaspoon salt
6 tablespoons (¾ stick) unsalted butter, softened
⅔ cup firmly packed light brown sugar

1 egg
1 teaspoon pure vanilla extract
¾ cup unsweetened applesauce
¼ cup firmly packed chopped pitted dates (I use the prechopped, presugared kind; break up large pieces, if necessary)
¼ cup raisins
⅓ cup finely chopped walnuts

1. Preheat the oven to 350 degrees. Line 12 muffin tins with paper liners or butter and flour the tins; set aside.

2. In a small bowl, whisk together the flour, cinnamon, ginger, baking powder, baking soda, and salt; set aside.

3. In a medium bowl, beat the butter until light and fluffy with an electric mixer on high speed. Gradually beat in the sugar. Lower the mixer speed to medium. Beat in the egg and the vanilla. Lower the mixer speed to low. Alternately beat in the flour mixture and the applesauce, just until blended. Fold in the chopped dates, raisins, and walnuts.

4. Spoon the batter into the prepared muffin tins.

5. Bake until the tops of the cupcakes are springy when lightly pressed with a fingertip, about 20 minutes. Cool for 15 minutes in the muffin tins on a wire rack.

Hazelnut cupcakes

Ground hazelnuts provide a macaroonlike quality, which can be furthered by the addition of raspberry or apricot preserves spread on baked, cooled, and halved cupcakes.

Makes 12 cupcakes

1 cup all-purpose flour
1½ teaspoons baking powder
⅛ teaspoon salt
½ cup (1 stick) unsalted butter, softened
¾ cup sugar

2 eggs
½ teaspoon pure vanilla extract
¼ teaspoon pure almond extract
½ cup milk
1 cup plus 1 tablespoon finely ground unblanched hazelnuts

1. Preheat the oven to 350 degrees. Line 12 muffin tins with paper liners or butter and flour the tins; set aside.

2. In a small bowl, whisk together the flour, baking powder, and salt; set aside.

3. In a medium bowl with an electric mixer on high speed, beat the butter, sugar, eggs, and vanilla and almond extracts until well blended, about 2 minutes. The mixture may curdle; don't worry!

4. Add the flour mixture and the milk. Beat on medium speed until the batter is smooth, about 1 minute. Fold in the ground hazelnuts.

5. Spoon the batter into the prepared muffin tins.

6. Bake until the cupcakes are springy when lightly pressed with a fingertip, about 20 minutes. The tops will probably not be colored, but the bottoms and sides will be. Let them cool in the tins on a wire rack.

ORANGE–BANANA CUPCAKES

The orange and banana flavors are well balanced in these moist cupcakes, neither one overpowering the other. Top them with Vanilla or Orange Buttercream.

Makes 12 cupcakes

1⅓ cups all-purpose flour
½ teaspoon baking powder
½ teaspoon baking soda
¼ teaspoon salt
½ cup (1 stick) unsalted butter, softened
⅔ cup sugar
2 eggs

½ cup mashed ripe banana (1 large banana)
Grated zest of 1 orange (about 1 tablespoon)
⅓ cup fresh orange juice
1 tablespoon orange liqueur (optional)

1. Preheat the oven to 350 degrees. Line 12 muffin tins with paper liners or butter and flour the tins; set aside.

2. In a small bowl, whisk together the flour, baking powder, baking soda, and salt; set aside.

3. In a medium bowl, beat the butter until light and fluffy with an electric mixer on high speed; gradually beat in the sugar until very light and fluffy. Lower the mixer speed to medium. Beat in the eggs, one at a time, then beat in the banana and orange zest. Lower the mixer speed to low. Beat in the flour mixture alternately with the orange juice and liqueur, just until blended.

4. Spoon the batter into the prepared muffin tins.

5. Bake until the tops of the cupcakes are golden and springy when lightly pressed with a fingertip, about 20 minutes. Cool for 15 minutes in the muffin tins on a wire rack. Transfer the cupcakes to the wire rack and cool completely.

APPLE-WHOLE-WHEAT CUPCAKES

Serve these maple-sweetened cupcakes with Cinnamon Glaze or Maple Whipped Cream. Top with an unpeeled apple wedge that's been dipped in lemon juice, or a drift of cinnamon sugar.

Makes 12 cupcakes

⅓ cup firmly packed dark brown sugar
½ cup maple syrup
6 tablespoons (¾ stick) unsalted butter, softened
2 eggs
1 teaspoon pure vanilla extract
¾ cup all-purpose flour

½ cup whole-wheat flour
1 teaspoon ground cinnamon
½ teaspoon baking powder
½ teaspoon baking soda
⅛ teaspoon salt
1 Granny Smith or other tart apple, peeled, cored, and chopped fine (about 1 cup)

1. Preheat the oven to 350 degrees. Line 12 muffin tins with paper liners or butter and flour the tins; set aside.

2. In a medium bowl with an electric mixer on high speed, beat the sugar, maple syrup, and butter until they are well blended and smooth. Lower the mixer speed to medium. Beat in the eggs and the vanilla.

3. In a small bowl, whisk together the all-purpose and whole-wheat flours, cinnamon, baking powder, baking soda, and salt; add to the creamed butter mixture and beat with the mixer on low speed, just until blended. Add the chopped apple to the batter. Beat to break down the apples slightly, about ½ minute.

4. Spoon the batter into the prepared muffin tins.

5. Bake until the tops of the cupcakes are golden and springy when lightly pressed with a fingertip, about 20 minutes. Cool completely in the muffin tins on a wire rack.

BANANA-NUT CUPCAKES

For a treat reminiscent of chocolate-covered bananas, split these moist cupcakes and fill them with vanilla, chocolate, or banana ice cream and a couple of firm banana slices; top with Chocolate Satin Glaze and refreeze. If desired, miniature chocolate chips can be substituted for all or part of the nuts.

Makes 12 cupcakes

¾ cup finely chopped walnuts
1½ cups all-purpose flour
¾ teaspoon baking powder
¾ teaspoon baking soda
¼ teaspoon salt
¾ cup mashed ripe banana (about 1½ medium bananas)

6 tablespoons plain yogurt
1 teaspoon pure vanilla extract
½ cup (1 stick) unsalted butter, softened
¾ cup sugar
1 egg
1 egg yolk

1. Preheat the oven to 350 degrees. While the oven preheats, toast the nuts in a cake pan (see page 26); set them aside to cool while preparing the rest of the batter.

2. Line 12 muffin tins with paper liners or butter and flour the tins; set aside.

3. In a small bowl, whisk together the flour, baking powder, baking soda, and salt; set aside. In a second small bowl, combine the mashed banana, yogurt, and vanilla; set aside.

4. In a medium bowl, beat the butter until light and fluffy with an electric mixer on high speed. Gradually beat in the sugar, beating after each addition. Continue beating until the mixture is very light and fluffy. Lower the mixer speed to medium. Beat in the egg, then the egg yolk. Lower the mixer speed to low. Beat in the flour mixture alternately with the banana mixture, just until blended. Stir in the nuts.

5. Spoon the batter into the prepared muffin tins.

6. Bake until the tops of the cupcakes are golden, springy when lightly pressed with a fingertip, but still slightly moist on top, 20 to 25 minutes. Cool for 15 minutes in the muffin tins on a wire rack. Transfer to the wire rack to cool completely.

Marzipan cupcakes

Moist and rich, these almond-flavored cupcakes are delicious simply layered with preserves, or topped with a lemon or chocolate frosting. Or fill and frost with White Chocolate Frosting, then decorate with toasted sliced almonds. For a more elaborate combination, brush the cupcakes with Apricot Glaze, top with a round of marzipan, then coat with Bittersweet Ganache.

Makes 12 cupcakes

⅓ cup all-purpose flour
½ teaspoon baking powder
Large pinch salt
⅔ cup sugar
½ cup (1 stick) unsalted butter, softened

1 package (7 ounces) almond paste
4 eggs
1 tablespoon kirsch, rum, or orange liqueur
¼ teaspoon pure almond extract (optional)

1. Preheat the oven to 350 degrees. Line 12 muffin tins with paper liners or butter and flour the tins; set aside.

2. In a cup, whisk together the flour, baking powder, and salt; set aside.

3. In a medium bowl, beat the sugar, butter, and almond paste with an electric mixer on high speed until light and fluffy. Beat in the eggs, liqueur, and extract. Lower the mixer speed to low. Beat in the flour mixture just until blended. Do not overbeat.

4. Spoon the batter into the prepared muffin tins.

5. Bake until the tops of the cupcakes are golden and springy when lightly pressed with a fingertip, 20 to 22 minutes. Cool for 15 minutes in the muffin tins on a wire rack.

BUTTERSCOTCH-PECAN CUPCAKES

Delicious with Butterscotch Glaze/Frosting or Lemon Buttercream.

Makes 12 cupcakes

½ cup pecans
1⅓ cups all-purpose flour
½ teaspoon baking powder
½ teaspoon baking soda
¼ teaspoon salt
½ cup (1 stick) unsalted butter, softened

¾ cup firmly packed dark brown sugar
2 eggs
2 teaspoons pure vanilla extract
½ cup milk
½ cup butterscotch pieces

1. Line 12 muffin tins with paper liners or butter and flour the tins; set aside.

2. Preheat the oven to 350 degrees. While the oven preheats, toast the pecans on a baking sheet until they are golden. Let cool, then coarsely break into pieces with your fingers; set aside.

3. In a small bowl, whisk together the flour, baking powder, baking soda, and salt; set aside.

4. In a medium bowl, beat the butter with an electric mixer on high speed until light and fluffy. Gradually add the sugar, beating after each addition, and continue beating until the mixture is very light and fluffy. Lower the mixer speed to medium. Beat in the eggs, one at a time, then beat in the vanilla. Lower the mixer speed to low. Beat in the flour mixture alternately with the milk, just until blended. Fold in the pecan and butterscotch pieces.

5. Spoon the batter into the prepared muffin tins.

6. Bake until the tops of the cupcakes are firm and springy, about 20 minutes. Cool in the tins on a wire rack.

DATE-NUT CUPCAKES

These cupcakes are richly endowed with the flavor of orange, from both orange zest and juice. They can be served simply with just a sprinkling of confectioners' sugar. Or, top them with Cream Cheese Frosting, Orange Buttercream, or Browned Butter Frosting.

Makes 12 cupcakes

1 1/3 cups all-purpose flour
1 teaspoon ground cinnamon
1/2 teaspoon baking powder
1/2 teaspoon baking soda
1/4 teaspoon salt
1/2 cup (1 stick) unsalted butter, softened
1/2 cup firmly packed light and/or dark brown sugar
1/4 cup honey

1 egg
1 egg yolk
1 teaspoon grated orange zest
1 teaspoon pure vanilla extract
1/2 cup fresh orange juice
1/2 cup firmly packed chopped pitted dates (I use the prechopped, pre-sugared kind; break up large pieces, if necessary)
1/2 cup finely chopped walnuts

1. Preheat the oven to 350 degrees. Line 12 muffin tins with paper liners or butter and flour the tins; set aside.

2. In a small bowl, whisk together the flour, cinnamon, baking powder, baking soda, and salt; set aside.

3. In a medium bowl, beat the butter until light and fluffy with an electric mixer on high speed; gradually beat in the sugar and honey until very light and fluffy. Lower the mixer speed to medium. Beat in the egg and egg yolk, then the orange zest and vanilla. Lower the mixer speed to low. Beat in the flour mixture alternately with the orange juice, just until blended. Stir in the dates and nuts.

4. Spoon the batter into the prepared muffin tins.

5. Bake until the tops of the cupcakes are golden and springy when lightly pressed with a fingertip, 20 to 25 minutes. Cool in the muffin tins on a wire rack.

PEANUT BUTTER CUPCAKES

Delicious with Cocoa Frosting or with Chocolate–Peanut Butter Frosting. If you really love peanut butter, add the filling from Peanut Butter Cups (page 158) before baking.

Makes 12 cupcakes

1⅓ cups all-purpose flour
½ teaspoon baking powder
½ teaspoon baking soda
Large pinch salt
¾ cup firmly packed dark brown sugar
⅓ cup peanut butter (not the natural kind; I use chunky)

6 tablespoons (¾ stick) unsalted butter, softened
2 eggs
1 teaspoon pure vanilla extract
½ cup milk

1. Preheat the oven to 350 degrees. Line 12 muffin tins with paper liners or butter and flour the tins; set aside.

2. In a small bowl, whisk together the flour, baking powder, baking soda, and salt; set aside.

3. In a medium bowl, beat the brown sugar, peanut butter, and butter until light with an electric mixer on high speed. Beat in the eggs and vanilla. Lower the mixer speed to low. Alternately beat in the flour mixture and the milk, just until blended.

4. Spoon the batter into the prepared muffin tins.

5. Bake until the tops of the cupcakes are springy when lightly pressed with a fingertip, about 20 minutes. Cool for 5 minutes in the muffin tins on a wire rack.

LINZER CHEWIES

A macaroon "top hat" decorates these jam-filled cupcakes. To add a nice counterpoint to the cookielike topping, choose a tangy unsweetened jam, such as apricot or raspberry. These go well with fruit teas.

Makes 12 cupcakes

MACAROON TOPPING
1 cup walnuts, pecans, almonds, or
  hazelnuts, or a combination
¼ cup sugar
1 egg white

BATTER
1 cup all-purpose flour
1 teaspoon baking powder
⅛ teaspoon salt

¼ cup (½ stick) unsalted butter,
  softened
⅔ cup sugar
1 egg
1 teaspoon pure vanilla extract
¼ teaspoon pure almond extract
½ cup sour cream
½ cup apricot or raspberry jam,
  preferably unsweetened, large
  pieces of fruit chopped, if necessary

1. Preheat the oven to 350 degrees. Line 12 muffin tins with paper liners or generously butter and flour the tins; set aside. (Because of the sticky macaroon mixture and the preserves, nonstick tins are helpful though not obligatory.)

2. To make the macaroon topping, combine the nuts and the sugar in the work bowl of a food processor. Cover and process until the nuts are finely ground. Transfer the nut mixture to a small bowl; add the egg white and mix until well blended. The topping will be soft and very sticky. Set aside.

3. To make the batter, whisk together the flour, baking powder, and salt in a small bowl; set aside.

4. In a medium bowl, beat the butter until light and fluffy with an electric mixer on high speed; gradually beat in the sugar until very light and fluffy. Lower the mixer speed to medium. Beat in the egg, then the vanilla and almond extracts.

5. Lower the mixer speed to low. Alternately beat in the flour mixture and the sour cream, beginning and ending with the flour mixture and beating just until blended. Spoon the batter into the prepared tins, smoothing the tops even.

6. Carefully divide the preserves among the portions of batter, avoiding the sides of the tins. Top each portion of batter with a mound of topping, pressing it in lightly.

7. Bake until the topping is set and the tops of the cupcakes are golden brown and soft but springy, 25 to 35 minutes. Let cool in the tins on a wire rack. Carefully loosen the cupcakes around the sides of the tins with a small knife.

ORANGE CUPCAKES

Top these with Orange Glaze, if desired.

Makes 12 cupcakes

1 cup all-purpose flour
½ teaspoon baking powder
½ teaspoon baking soda
¼ teaspoon salt
½ cup (1 stick) unsalted butter,
  softened
⅔ cup sugar

2 eggs
½ cup sour cream or plain yogurt
Grated zest of 1 orange (about 1
  tablespoon)
1 tablespoon orange liqueur
  (optional)

1. Preheat the oven to 350 degrees. Line 12 muffin tins with paper liners or butter and flour the tins; set aside.

2. In a small bowl, whisk together the flour, baking powder, baking soda, and salt; set aside.

3. In a medium bowl, beat the butter until light and fluffy with an electric mixer on high speed; gradually beat in the sugar, beating after each addition, and continue beating until the mixture is very light and fluffy. Lower the mixer speed to medium. Beat in the eggs,

one at a time, then beat in the sour cream, orange zest, and liqueur. Lower the mixer speed to low. Beat in the flour mixture, just until blended.

4. Spoon the batter into the prepared muffin tins.

5. Bake until the tops of the cupcakes are golden and springy when lightly pressed with a fingertip, about 20 minutes. Cool for 15 minutes in the muffin tins on a wire rack.

PINEAPPLE UPSIDE-DOWN CAKELETS

The classic cake recipe in miniature. As the cupcakes bake, the pineapple juice melds with the brown sugar and butter, to make a fruity caramel topping. If maraschino cherries offend you, be sure to replace them with other red fruits, such as dried cherries or fresh or dried cranberries; the little boost of color really makes a difference! Canned or poached dried apricot halves may be used in place of the pineapple.

Makes 12 cupcakes

UPSIDE-DOWN LAYER
3 tablespoons unsalted butter, melted
½ cup firmly packed light brown sugar
1 can (16 ounces) unsweetened pineapple slices packed in pineapple juice, drained (reserve the pineapple juice for the cake layer)
6 maraschino cherries, drained and halved, OR ⅓ cup dried cherries or fresh or dried cranberries

CAKE LAYER
1 cup all-purpose flour
½ teaspoon baking powder
½ teaspoon baking soda
⅛ teaspoon salt
6 tablespoons (¾ stick) unsalted
  butter, softened

⅔ cup sugar
2 eggs
1 teaspoon pure vanilla extract
Reserved pineapple juice plus milk, if
  necessary, to make ⅓ cup

1. Preheat the oven to 350 degrees. Butter 12 muffin tins; set aside.

2. To make the upside-down layer, spoon the melted butter into the muffin tins; sprinkle the brown sugar in an even layer over the melted butter. Halve six of the pineapple slices; curl each slice into an arc and press one arc into each muffin tin. Cut the remaining pineapple slices into pieces; add the pieces to the arcs in the muffin tins, to make complete circles. Place the cherry halves, cut sides up, in the center of the circles.

3. To make the cake layer, whisk together the flour, baking powder, baking soda, and salt in a small bowl; set aside.

4. In a medium bowl, beat the butter until light and fluffy with an electric mixer on high speed; gradually beat in the sugar, beating after each addition, and continue beating until the mixture is very light and fluffy. Lower the mixer speed to medium. Beat in the eggs, one at a time, then the vanilla extract.

5. Lower the mixer speed to low. Alternately beat in the flour mixture and the pineapple

juice, beginning and ending with the flour mixture and beating just until blended. Spoon the batter into the prepared tins, smoothing the tops until even.

6. Bake until the tops of the cupcakes are golden brown and soft but springy, about 20 minutes. Let stand in the tins on a wire rack for 5 minutes. Gently run a knife around the rim of each tin, to loosen the cupcakes. Carefully invert the cupcakes onto a large plate. Serve warm or at room temperature with dollops of unsweetened whipped cream, flavored with a dash of vanilla, if desired.

CRANBERRY–APRICOT CONFETTI CAKES

Doubly blessed with the tang of fresh cranberries and dried California apricots, these cupcakes become fancifully speckled as they bake. They're at their most flavorful after a day or two of mellowing.

Makes 12 cupcakes

FRUITED SUGAR
½ cup whole fresh or frozen cranberries (do not thaw if frozen)
12 California dried apricots
¼ cup sugar

BATTER
1⅓ cups all-purpose flour
½ teaspoon baking powder
½ teaspoon baking soda

¼ teaspoon salt
Juice of 1 tangerine or ½ navel orange, plus enough buttermilk to make ½ cup
½ cup (1 stick) unsalted butter, softened
⅔ cup sugar
2 egg yolks
Grated zest of 1 tangerine or ½ navel orange

1. Preheat the oven to 350 degrees. Line 12 muffin tins with paper liners or butter and flour the tins; set aside.

2. To make the fruited sugar, combine the cranberries, apricots, and sugar in the work bowl of a food processor. Cover and pulse-chop until the fruit is ground and well distributed throughout the sugar. The sugar will look like wet sand—only bright magenta!

3. To make the batter, whisk together the flour, baking powder, baking soda, and salt in a small bowl; set aside. Place the tangerine juice in a 1-cup measure; add enough buttermilk to make 1/2 cup liquid; set aside.

4. In a medium bowl with an electric mixer on high speed, beat the butter until light and fluffy. Gradually add the sugar, beating after each addition, and continue beating until the mixture is very light and fluffy. Lower the mixer speed to medium. Beat in the egg yolks, then the grated tangerine zest.

5. Lower the mixer speed to low. Alternately beat in the flour mixture with the buttermilk-juice mixture, just until blended.

6. Spoon the batter into the prepared tins.

7. Bake until the tops of the cupcakes are soft and springy and just starting to turn golden around the edges, 20 to 25 minutes. Cool in the tins on a wire rack.

Special-Occasion Cupcakes, Including Hidden Treasures

his chapter elevates cupcakes from homey to haute. Featured here are elegant presentations worthy of a dinner party, special flavors to celebrate special times, and Hidden Treasures, cupcakes with special fillings baked right into the batter. For a more dramatic dessert, the cupcakes can be napped with a sauce—such as *crème anglaise,* raspberry *coulis,* or ganache—or with lightly whipped cream.

MOM'S BIRTHDAY CUPCAKES

My mother's favorite confection is marzipan, but she also loves chocolate, so I combined the two flavors with a fruit that goes well with both—sour cherries. The chocolate-cake base was inspired by the Reine de Saba recipe from Julia Child's Mastering the Art of French Cooking, volume I. Although the baked cupcakes may seem underdone, they firm up quite a bit as they cool, leaving a fudgy center.

Makes 12 cupcakes

¼ cup canned sour cherries, drained (reserve ¼ cup syrup for melting with the chocolate)

¼ pound semisweet or bittersweet chocolate

2 ounces blanched almonds

⅔ cup sugar

⅔ cup all-purpose flour

¼ teaspoon baking powder

1 package (7 ounces) almond paste

½ cup (1 stick) unsalted butter, softened

3 eggs, separated
Pinch salt
I tablespoon cherry, raspberry, or
cassis liqueur (optional)

I recipe Chocolate Satin Glaze (page 241)
12 sour cherries, drained on paper towels, for garnish

1. Preheat the oven to 350 degrees. Line 12 muffin tins with paper liners or butter and flour the tins; set aside.

2. Chop the canned cherries and set aside. In a small saucepan over low heat, melt the chocolate with the reserved·1/4 cup of cherry juice. Let the mixture stand while preparing the rest of the batter.

3. In the work bowl of a food processor, grind the almonds with 2 tablespoons of the sugar; set aside. In a small bowl, whisk together the flour and baking powder; set aside.

4. Cut the almond paste into twenty-four equal pieces; roll each piece into a ball, then flatten into a disk. Wrap twelve of the disks in plastic wrap. (They'll be used after the cupcakes are baked.)

5. In a medium bowl, beat the butter and the remaining sugar with an electric mixer on high speed; beat until light and fluffy. Beat in the egg yolks, one at a time. Lower the mixer speed to low. Beat in the melted chocolate, then the ground almonds and chopped cherries. Beat in the flour mixture just until blended.

6. In a small bowl with the electric mixer on high speed, beat the egg whites and salt until the mixture forms stiff but not dry peaks. Fold the beaten egg whites into the chocolate batter.

7. Spoon half of the batter into the prepared muffin tins. Top with twelve of the almond-paste disks. Spoon the remaining batter over the almond paste.

8. Bake until the tops of the cupcakes are springy but the centers are still very wobbly, about 15 minutes. Do not overbake; the centers will firm up as the cupcakes cool. Cool for 15 minutes in the muffin tins on a wire rack. Unmold and let cool completely on the rack. Remove the paper liners, if used. (The cupcakes may be prepared a day in advance; do not remove the paper liners until you are ready to glaze them.)

9. Brush the cooled cupcakes with the liqueur; top with the remaining almond-paste disks. Place the cupcakes on the wire rack over a sheet of aluminum foil.

10. Pour the Chocolate Satin Glaze over the cupcakes. Reuse any glaze that drips onto the foil, to cover the uncoated areas of the cupcakes. Garnish with the whole cherries. Let stand until the glaze hardens.

CHOCOLATE–CHEESE–CAKE CUPCAKES

A dollop of chocolate chip–studded filling perches atop each cupcake, so rich that no frosting is needed. It's important to use ⅓ cup muffin tins, since the batter is abundant and overflows a bit.

Makes 12 cupcakes

CHEESE FILLING
¾ cup semisweet chocolate pieces
4 ounces cream cheese, softened
2 tablespoons sugar
1 egg yolk
½ teaspoon pure vanilla extract
1 teaspoon all-purpose flour
Pinch salt

CHOCOLATE BATTER
1 cup all-purpose flour

⅔ cup sugar
¼ cup unsweetened cocoa powder
½ teaspoon baking powder
½ teaspoon baking soda
¼ teaspoon salt
½ cup milk
⅓ cup flavorless vegetable oil
1 egg
1 teaspoon pure vanilla extract

1. Preheat the oven to 350 degrees. Line twelve ⅓-cup muffin tins with paper liners; set aside.

2. To make the cheese filling, melt ¼ cup of the chocolate pieces in a small heavy saucepan over low heat, or in the microwave (see page 22). Let cool. In a small bowl, with a large sturdy spoon, beat the cream cheese until it is light. Beat in the sugar and warm chocolate, then the egg yolk, vanilla, flour, and salt. Stir in the remaining ½ cup chocolate pieces; set aside.

3. To make the batter, whisk together the flour, sugar, cocoa, baking powder, baking soda, and salt in a medium bowl. Add the milk, oil, egg, and vanilla and beat until blended.

4. Spoon the batter into the prepared muffin tins. Top with the cream cheese mixture.

5. Bake until the tops of the cupcakes are firm and springy and the cheese filling is set, about 20 minutes. Cool in the tins on a wire rack.

PECAN-PIE CUPCAKES

A gooey pecan filling peeks out through the tops of these golden cupcakes. Vary the filling according to your preference: Dark corn syrup and dark brown sugar impart a deeper caramel flavor than light corn syrup and granulated sugar. Either way, a dollop of rum-flavored whipped cream makes a nice accompaniment.

Makes 12 cupcakes

BATTER
1 cup all-purpose flour
½ teaspoon baking powder
½ teaspoon baking soda
⅛ teaspoon salt
6 tablespoons (¾ stick) unsalted butter, softened
⅔ cup sugar
1 egg
1 egg yolk
1 tablespoon rum (optional)
1 teaspoon pure vanilla extract

⅓ cup sour cream

PECAN-PIE FILLING
1 egg
⅓ cup light or dark corn syrup
3 tablespoons granulated or firmly packed dark brown sugar
2 tablespoons (¼ stick) unsalted butter, melted
½ teaspoon pure vanilla extract
Pinch salt
½ cup chopped pecans

1. Preheat the oven to 350 degrees. Line 12 muffin tins with paper liners or butter and flour the tins; set aside.

2. To make the batter, whisk together the flour, baking powder, baking soda, and salt in a small bowl; set aside.

3. In a medium bowl, beat the butter until light and fluffy with an electric mixer on high speed; gradually beat in the sugar until very light and fluffy. Lower the mixer speed to medium. Beat in the egg and the egg yolk, then beat in the rum and the vanilla. Lower the mixer speed to low. Beat in the flour mixture alternately with the sour cream, just until blended, beginning and ending with the flour mixture.

4. Spoon the batter into the prepared muffin tins. Bake for 10 minutes.

5. Meanwhile, to make the filling, lightly beat the egg with a fork in a small bowl. Beat in the corn syrup, sugar, butter, vanilla, and salt until well blended.

6. Working quickly, make a deep depression in the center of each mound of partially baked batter with a spoon. Evenly divide the pecans among the depressions, pressing down with the spoon. Carefully spoon the filling into the depressions, pressing down with the spoon so some of the filling sinks down into the batter.

7. Continue baking until the tops of the cupcakes are golden and springy and the edges of the filling are set but the centers are still a bit wobbly, about 15 minutes longer. Cool completely in the tins on a wire rack.

"Truffles"

These rough-hewn little treats are actually vanilla sponge cakes moistened with rum syrup, completely enrobed in a chocolate-cherry buttercream, then rolled in chopped chocolate. Because of the syrup and the buttercream, they keep well for several days. The cherry-cordial buttercream is also a delicious topping on its own, used as a frosting.

Makes 12 cupcakes

RUM SYRUP AND SOAKED CHERRIES
½ cup water
¼ cup dried sour cherries
½ cup sugar
⅓ cup rum
1 teaspoon rum extract (optional)

1 recipe Hot-Milk Sponge Cakes
 (page 76)

CHERRY-CORDIAL BUTTERCREAM
1 bar (3 ounces) bittersweet chocolate, chopped, or ½ cup (3 ounces)
 semisweet chocolate pieces
½ cup (1 stick) unsalted butter
2 cups confectioners' sugar, sifted if
 lumpy
½ cup unsweetened cocoa powder
Pinch salt
⅓ cup milk

3 tablespoons reserved rum syrup

2⅔ cups (about 14 ounces) finely chopped chocolate (see Note), chocolate cookie crumbs, or chocolate sprinkles

1. Prepare the rum syrup and soaked cherries: In a small saucepan over moderate heat, bring the water and cherries to a boil. Add the sugar and continue cooking for about 1½ minutes, or until the sugar dissolves. Remove from the heat. Let stand for about 30 minutes, or until tepid. Stir in the rum and rum extract. Set aside. (The syrup and cherries may be made several days in advance; transfer to a jar, cover, and keep in a cool place.) Just before using the cherries, remove them from the syrup, reserving the syrup, and chop the cherries.

2. Prepare the cherry-cordial buttercream: In a small heavy saucepan, combine the chocolate with 3 tablespoons of the butter. Melt over low heat, stirring occasionally.

3. In a medium bowl, combine the sugar, cocoa, salt, milk, and rum syrup. Beat with an electric mixer on medium speed until blended.

4. Beat in the melted chocolate mixture, then the remaining 5 tablespoons of butter, bit by bit, until blended and fluffy. Stir in the chopped cherries. The mixture will be thin.

5. Remove the paper liners from the cupcakes, if they were used. Brush syrup all over the cupcakes. Let stand about 15 minutes.

6. Place the chopped chocolate on a piece of plastic wrap. Working with one cupcake at a time, carefully dip it in the buttercream, spreading to coat all over, then drop the cupcake into the chopped chocolate. Use the plastic wrap to roll the cupcake around and

completely cover it with the chopped chocolate. Place the coated cupcakes on a waxed paper–lined cookie sheet. Let stand while preparing the remaining cupcakes. Refrigerate the cupcakes, loosely covered with plastic wrap. Bring to room temperature before serving.

Note: To chop chocolate, break into pieces and pulse-chop, in batches, in a food processor.

"CUPPUCCINOS"

Assembled and served in coffee cups, these whimsical versions of tiramisu combine layers of espresso-moistened sponge cakes with a rich mascarpone filling. Lightly whipped cream resembles the "foam."

Vary the liqueurs as desired, but try to include an orange liqueur, because its citrus perfume really enhances the flavor of the dessert. This is a rich dessert, best served in the afternoon or after a light meal.

Makes 12 cupcakes

SWEETENED ESPRESSO
¼ cup sugar
1 tablespoon instant espresso powder
1 cup strong brewed Italian- or
  French-roast coffee

¼ cup Kahlúa or other coffee liqueur
¼ cup triple sec or other orange
  liqueur

MASCARPONE FILLING
4 egg yolks
¾ cup sugar
¼ cup port, sweet sherry, or blackberry brandy
¼ cup triple sec or other orange
  liqueur
1 pound mascarpone cheese (or one
  17½ ounce container)
1 cup heavy or whipping cream
1 teaspoon pure vanilla extract

1 recipe Hot-Milk Sponge Cakes
  (page 76)

WHIPPED-CREAM TOPPING
1 cup heavy or whipping cream
2 tablespoons sugar

Ground cinnamon or unsweetened
  cocoa, for dusting on top of the assembled desserts

1. Prepare the sweetened espresso: In a small saucepan, add the sugar and espresso powder to the hot coffee. Place over low heat and stir until the sugar and espresso are dissolved. The coffee should be quite strong, just on the cusp of bitterness. If necessary, add a bit more coffee powder. Remove from the heat. Stir in the Kahlúa and triple sec. Set aside.

2. Prepare the mascarpone filling: In a heatproof bowl that will fit snugly over a pan of simmering water, beat the egg yolks until blended, then slowly beat in the sugar, port, and triple sec.

3. Using a wire whisk, beat the egg mixture constantly and vigorously over the simmering water until it thickens and expands in volume. Immediately remove from the heat. Continue whisking until the mixture is completely cooled.

4. In a medium bowl, whisk the mascarpone to aerate it and make it smooth. Fold in the beaten egg-yolk mixture.

5. In a small bowl with an electric mixer on medium speed, beat the cream with the vanilla until it holds soft peaks. Fold the whipped cream into the mascarpone mixture.

6. To assemble the desserts, remove the paper liners from the cupcakes, if used. Split each of the cupcakes into three layers. Place the bottom layers, cut sides up, in twelve 8-ounce coffee cups, large enough to hold the cupcakes with a border around them to accommodate the filling. Moisten with about one third of the sweetened espresso. Top with about one third of the mascarpone filling. Repeat the process with the middle cake layers, about one third of the espresso, and one third of the filling, gently pressing the cupcake layers into the first filling layers and using enough espresso to moisten the layers but not so much that it runs off the cake into the filling. Add the top cupcake layers, cut sides up, and brush with enough of the remaining espresso to moisten the cake but not so much that it runs off into the filling. (There may be a little espresso left over at the end—a nice reward for the dessert maker!) Top with the remaining filling, gently spreading, if necessary, to cover the cake. Cover the desserts loosely with plastic wrap and refrigerate them until shortly before serving time. (The desserts can be made a day or two ahead up to this point.)

7. Shortly before serving time, make the whipped-cream topping: In a small bowl with the electric mixer on medium speed, beat the cream with the sugar until it holds soft peaks. Gently swirl the whipped cream over the cupcakes to cover them completely, mounding the topping as much as possible to resemble the "foam" of a cappuccino. Dust with the cinnamon or cocoa powder. Place the coffee cups on saucers to serve.

Note: The recipe can be halved.

Coffee-Caramel Nut Cakes

These cupcakes, miniature versions of one of my favorite coffee cakes, are redolent with gooey swirls of macadamia-espresso caramel. Serve them with a light dusting of confectioners' sugar, or drizzle them with Espresso Glaze and top each one with a whole macadamia nut.

Makes 12 cupcakes

MACADAMIA-ESPRESSO CARAMEL
2 tablespoons firmly packed dark
   brown sugar
1 tablespoon granulated sugar
2 tablespoons heavy or whipping
   cream
1 tablespoon unsalted butter
1 tablespoon light corn syrup
1 teaspoon instant espresso
   powder

¼ cup very finely chopped
   macadamia nuts
¼ cup ground plain cookies, such as
   Petit Beurre or shortbread
¼ teaspoon ground cinnamon

BATTER
1 cup all-purpose flour
½ teaspoon baking powder
¼ teaspoon baking soda

¼ teaspoon salt

⅓ cup sour cream

1 teaspoon instant espresso powder
dissolved in 1 teaspoon hot water

1 teaspoon rum or brandy

1 teaspoon pure vanilla extract

6 tablespoons (¾ cup) unsalted butter, softened

⅔ cup firmly packed dark brown
sugar

1 egg

1 egg yolk

1. To make the macadamia-espresso caramel, combine the brown and granulated sugars, cream, butter, corn syrup, and espresso powder in a small heavy saucepan. Bring to
a boil over moderate heat, stirring often. Lower the heat and simmer, stirring often, for
3 minutes. Remove from the heat and stir in the nuts, ground cookies, and cinnamon.
Let cool. (This can be done ahead, even a day or two before; cover and refrigerate the
caramel until you are ready to use it.) The caramel will become gooey and thick as it cools.

2. Preheat the oven to 350 degrees. Line 12 muffin tins with paper liners or butter and
flour the tins set aside.

3. To make the batter, whisk together the flour, baking powder, baking soda, and salt in
a small bowl; set aside. In a cup, combine the sour cream, espresso dissolved in water,
rum, and vanilla; set aside.

4. In a medium bowl, beat the butter with an electric mixer on high speed until it is light
and fluffy. Gradually add the sugar, beating after each addition, and continue beating
until the mixture is very light and fluffy. Lower the mixer speed to medium. Add the egg
and egg yolk, beating well after each addition.

5. Lower the mixer speed to low. Alternately beat in the dry ingredients and the sour-cream mixture, beginning and ending with the dry ingredients and beating only until combined.

6. Spoon the batter into the prepared muffin tins. Divide the caramel into twelve equal blobs and press one blob into the top center of each portion of batter.

7. Bake until the filling bubbles up and the tops of the cupcakes are deeply colored and spring back when lightly pressed with a fingertip, about 20 minutes. Cool completely in the tins on a wire rack.

COCONUT SURPRISE CUPCAKES

This is the cupcake version of the Coconut Tunnel of Fudge Cake that appeared in my Coffee Cakes book. What a treat to discover bittersweet chocolate filling hiding in the middle of a dense coconut pound cake! Although the flavor of these cupcakes is complete on its own, Vanilla Buttercream sprinkled with toasted coconut and shaved chocolate makes a nice embellishment.

Makes 12 cupcakes

CHOCOLATE FUDGE FILLING
- ⅔ cup (4 ounces) semisweet chocolate pieces or ¼ pound semisweet or bittersweet chocolate, chopped
- 2 tablespoons heavy or whipping cream
- 1 tablespoon light corn syrup
- 1 tablespoon sugar

BATTER
- 1 cup all-purpose flour
- ½ teaspoon baking powder
- ⅛ teaspoon salt
- 1 teaspoon pure vanilla extract
- ⅛ teaspoon pure almond extract
- ⅓ cup milk
- 6 tablespoons (¾ stick) unsalted butter, softened

²⁄₃ cup sugar
1 egg
1 egg yolk

½ cup firmly packed sweetened flaked coconut (about 5 ounces)

1. Preheat the oven to 350 degrees. Line 12 muffin tins with paper liners or butter and flour the tins; set aside.

2. To make the filling, combine the chocolate, cream, corn syrup, and sugar in a small heavy saucepan. Place over moderately low heat and cook, stirring often, until the chocolate melts and the mixture is smooth. Remove from the heat. Set aside.

3. To make the batter, whisk together the flour, baking powder, and salt in a small bowl. Add the vanilla and almond extracts to the milk. Set the dry ingredients and the milk aside.

4. In a medium bowl, beat the butter with an electric mixer on high speed until light and fluffy. Gradually add the sugar, beating after each addition, and continue beating until the mixture is very light and fluffy. Lower the mixer speed to medium. Add the egg and the egg yolk, beating until blended. The mixture may look curdled; this is okay!

5. Lower the mixer speed to low. Alternately beat in the dry ingredients and the milk, beginning and ending with the dry ingredients and beating only until combined. Beat in the coconut.

6. Spoon about two thirds of the batter into the prepared tins. Using the bottom of a large spoon, make a depression in the center of each mound of batter. Spoon the fudge

filling into the depressions, avoiding the sides of the tins and pressing the filling in slightly. Top with the remaining batter, carefully spreading it to cover and enclose the filling completely.

7. Bake until the tops of the cupcakes are golden brown and springy when lightly pressed with a fingertip, about 25 minutes. Cool completely in the tins on a wire rack.

COCONUT-ALMOND CUPCAKES

A toasted almond-and-coconut filling nestles within moist orange batter. Top with White-Chocolate Frosting or Orange Buttercream. Or glaze with Bittersweet Ganache.

Makes 12 cupcakes

COCONUT-ALMOND FILLING
2 tablespoons blanched slivered almonds
3 ounces cream cheese, softened
2 tablespoons sugar
½ cup sweetened flaked coconut
½ teaspoon pure vanilla extract
⅛ teaspoon pure almond extract

BATTER
1 cup all-purpose flour

¾ teaspoon baking powder
½ teaspoon baking soda
⅛ teaspoon salt
6 tablespoons (¾ stick) unsalted butter, softened
¾ cup sugar
2 eggs
1 teaspoon grated orange zest
1 teaspoon pure vanilla extract
⅓ cup fresh orange juice

1. Line 12 muffin tins with paper liners or butter and flour the tins; set aside.

2. To make the filling, preheat the oven to 350 degrees. As the oven preheats, toast the almonds on a baking sheet until they are golden. Let them cool while preparing the rest of the filling.

3. In a small bowl, beat the cream cheese until it is light with a large sturdy spoon. Beat in the sugar, the coconut, and the vanilla and almond extracts. Stir in the toasted almonds. Set aside.

4. To make the batter, whisk together the flour, baking powder, baking soda, and salt in a small bowl; set aside.

5. In a medium bowl, beat the butter with an electric mixer on high speed until light and fluffy. Gradually beat in the sugar, beating after each addition, and continue beating until the mixture is very light and fluffy. Lower the mixer speed to medium. Beat in the eggs, one at a time, then beat in the orange zest and vanilla. Lower the mixer speed to low. Beat in the flour mixture alternately with the orange juice, just until blended.

6. Spoon half of the batter into the prepared muffin tins. Spoon a dollop of the coconut filling in the center of each portion of batter. Top with the remaining batter, smoothing it over the filling.

7. Bake until the tops of the cupcakes are golden and springy, about 20 minutes. Cool in the tins on a wire rack.

GRAND MARNIER OUNCECAKES

Too dainty to be called pound cakes, these triple-orange cupcakes boast more than their weight in tender perfection. Brushed with a tangy glaze that makes them super moist and citrusy, they're delicious with tiny scoops of orange sherbet and vanilla ice cream.

Makes 12 cupcakes

CUPCAKES
1½ cups all-purpose flour
1 teaspoon baking powder
¼ teaspoon salt
¾ cup (1½ sticks) unsalted butter,
  softened
1 cup sugar
3 eggs
3 tablespoons orange liqueur (Grand
Marnier, Cointreau, or triple sec)
2 teaspoons grated orange zest
¼ cup fresh orange juice

FRESH ORANGE GLAZE
¼ cup fresh orange juice
2 tablespoons orange liqueur
1 tablespoon sugar

1. To make the cupcakes, preheat the oven to 350 degrees. Line 12 muffin tins with paper liners or butter and flour the tins; set aside.

2. In a small bowl, whisk together the flour, baking powder, and salt; set aside.

3. In a medium bowl, beat the butter with an electric mixer on high speed until light and fluffy. Gradually beat in the sugar, beating after each addition, and continue beating until the mixture is very light and fluffy. Lower the mixer speed to medium. Beat in the eggs, one at a time, beating well after each addition, then beat in the liqueur, orange zest, and orange juice. The mixture will look disastrously curdled but don't worry!

4. Lower the mixer speed to low. Beat in the flour mixture just until it is absorbed.

5. Spoon the batter into the prepared tins.

6. Bake until the cupcakes shrink from the sides of the tins and the tops are flecked with gold, 25 to 30 minutes. Let stand in the tins on a wire rack for 10 minutes.

7. Meanwhile, to prepare the glaze, combine the orange juice, liqueur, and sugar in a small saucepan. Bring to a boil over moderate heat. Lower the heat and simmer until the mixture forms a light syrup, about 5 minutes.

8. If you've used paper liners, carefully peel them away. Return the cupcakes, right side up, to the rack; place the rack over a piece of waxed paper or aluminum foil. Brush the syrup all over the warm cupcakes. Let them cool completely.

PEANUT BUTTER CUPS

A grainy dollop of peanut-butter filling nestles within these fudgy cupcakes. Top them with Whipped Milk-Chocolate Frosting or serve them on a plate napped with whipped cream and Microwave Fudge Sauce for a wickedly elegant dessert.

Makes 12 cupcakes

FILLING
6 tablespoons creamy or chunky peanut butter
1/4 cup granulated sugar

BATTER
1/3 cup unsweetened cocoa powder
1/4 cup hot water
1 cup all-purpose flour
1/2 teaspoon baking powder
1/4 teaspoon baking soda

1/8 teaspoon salt
6 tablespoons (3/4 stick) unsalted butter, softened
1/3 cup creamy or chunky peanut butter
3/4 cup firmly packed light brown sugar
2 egg yolks
1 teaspoon pure vanilla extract
1/3 cup milk

1. Preheat the oven to 350 degrees. Line 12 muffin tins with paper liners or butter and flour the tins; set aside.

2. To make the filling, combine the peanut butter and sugar in a small bowl until well blended. Set aside.

3. To make the batter, combine the cocoa powder and hot water in a cup until smooth; set aside. In a small bowl, whisk together the flour, baking powder, baking soda, and salt; set aside.

4. In a medium bowl with an electric mixer on high speed, beat the butter and peanut butter until light and creamy. Slowly beat in the sugar. Lower the mixer speed to medium; beat in the egg yolks, one at a time. Beat in the cocoa mixture, then the vanilla. Lower the mixer speed to low. Beat in the flour mixture alternately with the milk, beginning and ending with the flour and beating just until combined.

5. Spoon about two thirds of the batter into the prepared tins. Top with equal amounts of the peanut butter filling, then the remaining batter, smoothing the tops.

6. Bake until the tops of the cupcakes are cracked, the edges are springy, and the centers are still quite soft when lightly pressed with a fingertip, about 20 minutes. Cool in the tins on a wire rack.

LITTLE BOSTON CREAM PIES

These custard-filled cupcakes are diminutive versions of the all-American cake, topped with either chocolate frosting or a dusting of confectioners' sugar.

Makes 12 cupcakes

CUSTARD FILLING
1 cup milk
⅓ cup sugar
⅛ teaspoon salt
2 tablespoons cornstarch
2 egg yolks

1 teaspoon pure vanilla extract

1 recipe Hot-Milk Sponge Cakes
 (page 76)
½ recipe Cocoa Frosting (page 225)
 or sifted confectioners' sugar

1. To make the custard filling, combine about two thirds of the milk with the sugar and salt in a small heavy saucepan. Bring to a boil over moderate heat.

2. Pour the remaining milk into a small bowl; beat in the cornstarch, then the egg yolks.

3. Whisk a little of the hot milk into the egg-yolk mixture, whisking constantly. Bring the remaining milk in the saucepan back to a boil over moderate heat. Whisking constantly, pour the tempered egg mixture into the saucepan.

4. Cook, whisking constantly, until the mixture comes to a boil. Lower the heat; simmer for 1 minute longer, stirring constantly. Immediately remove the saucepan from the heat, pour the custard into a small bowl, and stir in the vanilla extract. Immediately cover the surface of the custard directly with plastic wrap. Refrigerate until cold, up to 24 hours.

5. Remove the paper liners from the cupcakes, if they were used. Split the cupcakes. Carefully fill them with the custard, replacing the tops. Gently spread the frosting over the cupcakes, or dust the tops with confectioners' sugar. Keep refrigerated until serving time, lightly covering the cupcakes with plastic wrap once the frosting has set.

Cupcakes for a Crowd

T|he larger-scale recipes included in this chapter are for those times when you're baking for a crowd: A child's birthday party, a holiday gathering, or an open house often calls for more than a dozen cup-cakes. Kids love cupcakes, so they're a natural choice for birthday and holiday parties. A birthday candle in each child's cupcake enables all the partygoers to get into the action. But don't let cupcakes' association with chil-dren stop you from serving them to adults, too. They're ideal for buffets because a platter will look neat even when a number of servings have been removed.

To finish the cupcakes, choose one of the many variations given in A Big Batch of Buttercream, or use a couple of smaller-quantity frostings.

PUMPKIN CUPCAKES

Don't be put off by the number of ingredients in this recipe. They combine quickly to produce a warmly spiced batter. Of course, these are a natural for Halloween parties or a Thanksgiving buffet. See chapter 10 for a few decorating ideas.

Makes 24 cupcakes

2½ cups all-purpose flour
2 teaspoons baking powder
1 teaspoon baking soda
½ teaspoon salt
2 teaspoons ground ginger
2 teaspoons ground cinnamon
½ teaspoon ground or grated
  nutmeg

½ teaspoon ground cloves
2 cups canned pumpkin purée (not
  pumpkin-pie filling)
4 eggs
⅔ cup vegetable oil
1½ cups sugar
⅔ cup milk

1. Adjust two oven racks in the upper and lower thirds of your oven. Preheat the oven to 350 degrees. Line 24 muffin tins with paper liners or butter and flour the tins; set aside.

2. In a large bowl, whisk together the flour, baking powder, baking soda, salt, ginger, cinnamon, nutmeg, and cloves. Set aside.

3. In the work bowl of a large food processor, combine the pumpkin, eggs, oil, sugar, and milk; process until well blended. (If you don't have a processor, beat everything together in a second large bowl.)

4. Pour the pumpkin mixture over the dry ingredients; beat with an electric mixer on high speed or stir vigorously with a heavy wooden spoon until well blended. Spoon the batter into the prepared tins.

5. Bake until the cupcakes spring back when lightly pressed with a fingertip, 20 to 25 minutes, switching the oven-rack levels of the pans after 15 minutes of baking. Cool in the tins on a wire rack.

CHOCOLATE CUPCAKES FOR A CROWD

These cupcakes are a guaranteed favorite with kids, whatever frosting they're teamed with.

Makes 24 cupcakes

½ cup hot water
¾ cup unsweetened cocoa powder
2½ cups all-purpose flour
2 teaspoons baking powder
1 teaspoon baking soda
½ teaspoon salt

1 cup (2 sticks) unsalted butter, softened
1½ cups sugar
4 eggs
1 tablespoon pure vanilla extract
1⅓ cups milk

1. Adjust two oven racks in the upper and lower thirds of your oven. Preheat the oven to 350 degrees. Line 24 muffin tins with paper liners or butter and flour the tins; set aside.

2. In a small bowl, combine the hot water and the cocoa powder until they form a smooth paste; set aside.

3. In a medium bowl, whisk together the flour, baking powder, baking soda, and salt; set aside.

4. In a large bowl, beat the butter with an electric mixer on high speed until light and fluffy. Gradually add the sugar, beating after each addition, until the mixture is very light and fluffy. Lower the mixer speed to medium. Beat in the eggs, two at a time, then the cocoa mixture and the vanilla extract.

5. Lower the mixer speed to low. Alternately beat in the flour mixture with the milk, just until blended. Spoon the batter into the prepared tins.

6. Bake until the tops of the cupcakes are soft but springy, 20 to 25 minutes, switching the oven-rack positions of the pans after 15 minutes of baking. Cool in the tins on a wire rack.

VANILLA CUPCAKES FOR A CROWD

Despite chocolate's universal allure, a substantial percentage of people prefer vanilla's intoxicating flavor and scent. To enhance the vanilla perfume of these cupcakes, substitute the vanilla sugar described below for plain sugar, in addition to the extract.

Makes 24 cupcakes

2½ cups all-purpose flour
1 tablespoon baking powder
½ teaspoon salt
1 cup (2 sticks) unsalted butter,
  softened

1¾ cups sugar (see Note)
4 eggs
1 tablespoon pure vanilla extract
1 cup milk

1. Adjust two oven racks in the upper and lower thirds of your oven. Preheat the oven to 350 degrees. Line 24 muffin tins with paper liners or butter and flour the tins; set aside.

2. In a medium bowl, whisk together the flour, baking powder, and salt; set aside.

3. In a large bowl, beat the butter until light and fluffy with an electric mixer on high speed; gradually beat in the sugar until very light and fluffy. Lower the mixer speed to medium. Beat in the eggs, two at a time, then the vanilla extract.

4. Lower the mixer speed to low. Alternately beat in the flour mixture with the milk, just until blended. Spoon the batter into the prepared tins.

5. Bake until the tops of the cupcakes are soft but springy, 20 to 25 minutes, switching the oven-rack positions of the pans after 15 minutes of baking. Cool in the tins on a wire rack.

Note: For a more pronounced vanilla flavor, make vanilla sugar: Bury a halved vanilla bean in a container of granulated sugar; cover tightly and let stand at least a few days. The sugar will become delicately scented with the vanilla. The vanilla bean can be reused.

CARROT CUPCAKES FOR A CROWD

These extra-moist cupcakes are traditionally topped with Cream Cheese Frosting. They can also be embellished with Cream Cheese Glaze. Vary the additions to the batter: Use golden raisins rather than dark ones for a tangier taste; substitute shredded coconut for all or part of the nuts.

Makes 24 cupcakes

2½ cups all-purpose flour
1⅔ cups sugar
2 teaspoons baking powder
2 teaspoons ground cinnamon
1 teaspoon salt
1⅓ cups vegetable oil
3 eggs
1 teaspoon baking soda
⅓ cup buttermilk

2 teaspoons pure vanilla extract
1 can (8 ounces) crushed pineapple
  in pineapple juice
⅔ cup finely chopped pecans or
  walnuts
⅓ cup golden or dark raisins
2 cups grated carrot (about ½ pound)

1. Adjust two oven racks in the upper and lower thirds of your oven. Preheat the oven to 350 degrees. Line 24 muffin tins with paper liners or butter and flour the tins; set aside.

2. In a large bowl, whisk together the flour, sugar, baking powder, cinnamon, and salt.

3. Add the oil and eggs. Combine the baking soda with the buttermilk; add it, and then the vanilla. Beat with an electric mixer on low speed until well blended, about 1 minute. Continue beating for 3 minutes longer. The batter will be very thick, almost gluey. Don't worry!

4. Stir the pineapple and its juice, pecans, raisins, and carrots into the batter until well distributed.

5. Pour the batter into the prepared tins. (For ease of pouring, transfer the batter to a pitcher.)

6. Bake until the tops of the cupcakes are springy and firm, 20 to 25 minutes, switching the oven-rack positions of the pans after 15 minutes of baking. Cool in the tins on a wire rack.

On the Light Side

O ne of the advantages of cupcakes is that they're already divided into small, easily divisible portions. For an even lighter approach to calories, cholesterol, and fat, choose from the handful of recipes provided here.

Since frosting is often the culprit in tipping the scales, a fat-free glaze or a sprinkling of confectioners' sugar is an easy way to reduce calories and fat. Billowy Frosting, made from beaten egg whites, is another suitable topping; its luxurious texture and bountiful swirls belie its low-fat profile.

CRANBERRY BURSTS

This highly unorthodox recipe, from Miriam and Keren Osman, uses a full 12-ounce bag of cranberries, bound in what will appear like an impossibly thick batter. During baking, the cranberries release their tangy juices, adding bursts of color and moistness to the cupcakes. Serve them with a side dollop of orange sorbet or vanilla frozen yogurt. Note that the cupcakes are quite low in fat, too.

Makes 12 cupcakes

1 tablespoon dry bread crumbs
1 ¼ cups all-purpose flour
1 teaspoon baking powder
⅛ teaspoon salt
1 cup sugar
¼ cup milk, at room temperature
2 eggs

3 tablespoons unsalted butter, softened
1 bag (yes, the whole 12 ounces!) fresh or frozen cranberries (don't thaw if frozen), rinsed, picked over, and well drained

1. Preheat the oven to 375 degrees. Line 12 muffin tins with paper liners. (Since these cupcakes exude juice, paper liners are necessary; a nonstick muffin pan makes matters

even simpler.) Sprinkle the bottom of each tin with some of the bread crumbs (these absorb excess juice); set aside.

2. In a small bowl, whisk together the flour, baking powder, and salt; set aside.

3. In a large bowl with an electric mixer on high speed, beat together the sugar, milk, eggs, and butter until blended. (There may still be flecks of butter throughout—this is okay.) Lower the mixer speed to low. Beat in the flour mixture, then the cranberries, breaking up some of the cranberries as they are added.

4. Spoon the cranberries and batter into the prepared tins, pushing the cranberries down.

5. Bake until the tops of the cupcakes are golden brown and the cranberries release their juice, about 30 minutes. Cool completely in the tins on a wire rack. Carefully loosen the cupcakes around the edges to remove them (the juices may make them stick). Store the cupcakes in a tightly closed container. They improve if left to mellow for at least a day. In fact, they will keep for several days.

Coconut Macaroon Cupcakes

Dense and chewy, these treats are half cupcake, half confection—and for confirmed coconut lovers only! For coconut-candy bar cupcakes, dip the bottoms in melted chocolate, then in chopped toasted almonds; let them dry on waxed paper. Or, serve the cupcakes on plates napped with Mango Coulis and/or puréed raspberries.

Makes 12 cupcakes

4 egg whites
¼ teaspoon salt
¼ teaspoon cream of tartar
⅔ cup sugar

1 teaspoon pure vanilla extract
½ teaspoon pure almond extract
⅓ cup all-purpose flour
2½ cups sweetened flaked coconut

1. Preheat the oven to 325 degrees. Line 12 muffin tins with paper liners; set aside.

2. In a medium bowl with an electric mixer on high speed, beat the egg whites, salt, and cream of tartar until foamy. Slowly beat in the sugar, 1 tablespoon at a time, and con-

tinue beating until the mixture forms stiff but not dry peaks. Beat in the vanilla and almond extracts.

3. Beat in the flour, then the coconut. The batter will be very white and very lumpy! Spoon the batter into the prepared tins.

4. Bake for 25 to 30 minutes, or until the tops are golden and springy when lightly pressed with a fingertip. The cupcakes will be a bit soft in the center. Because of their high proportion of moist coconut, these cupcakes will keep for at least a week if stored in a tightly closed container.

No-cholesterol Pumpkin Cupcakes

These cupcakes, miniature versions of my friend Jessica Feinleib's popular cake, are beautiful topped with her Dried-Cranberry Whip.

Makes 12 cupcakes

1 ⅓ cups all-purpose flour
1 teaspoon baking powder
1 teaspoon baking soda
¼ teaspoon salt
1 teaspoon ground cinnamon
½ teaspoon ground or grated nutmeg

¾ cup canned pumpkin purée (not pie filling)
¾ cup sugar
½ cup vegetable oil
4 egg whites

1. Preheat the oven to 350 degrees. Line 12 muffin tins with paper liners or spray the tins with vegetable cooking spray and flour them. Set aside.

2. In a small bowl, whisk together the flour, baking powder, baking soda, salt, cinnamon, and nutmeg; set aside.

3. In a medium bowl with an electric mixer on high speed, beat together the pumpkin, sugar, and oil. (The mixture will seem lumpy and curdled but will come together when the egg whites are added.) Beat in the egg whites, one at a time. Lower the mixer speed to low. Add the dry ingredients and continue beating for 30 seconds.

4. Spoon the batter into the prepared tins.

5. Bake until the cupcakes are golden and springy and firm when lightly pressed with a fingertip, 20 to 25 minutes. Cool in the tins on a wire rack.

Feather-Light Orange Cupcakes

These light cupcakes are made with only one egg yolk and 3 table-spoons of butter. Even when frosted, they contain just 151 calories and less than 4 grams of fat each. Trust Jim Fobel, author of Diet Feasts, to combine so much flavor with so little guilt!

Makes 12 cupcakes

CUPCAKES
1½ teaspoons grated orange zest
¼ cup fresh orange juice
3 tablespoons unsalted butter, melted
1 teaspoon pure vanilla extract
½ teaspoon orange extract
1 egg yolk
1 cup sifted cake flour (not self-rising)
⅔ cup sugar
1½ teaspoons baking powder
⅛ teaspoon salt
4 egg whites, at room temperature

⅛ teaspoon cream of tartar

FLUFFY ORANGE FROSTING
½ cup sugar
3 tablespoons water
1 egg white
⅛ teaspoon cream of tartar
Dash salt
1 teaspoon grated orange zest
½ teaspoon orange extract
2 drops red food coloring
2 drops yellow food coloring

1. To make the cupcakes, preheat the oven to 350 degrees. Line 12 muffin tins with paper liners or spray the tins with vegetable cooking spray and flour them. Set aside.

2. In a small bowl, combine the orange zest and juice, butter, vanilla and orange extracts, and egg yolk.

3. In a large bowl, combine the flour, $1/3$ cup of the sugar, baking powder, and salt. Add the orange-juice mixture and beat with a wire whisk until smooth and well blended. Set aside.

4. In a large bowl with an electric mixer on high speed, beat the egg whites and cream of tartar until foamy. Gradually add the remaining $1/3$ cup of sugar, 1 tablespoon at a time, beating until stiff peaks form. Gently stir one fourth of the egg whites into the orange mixture, then fold in the remainder, one third at a time.

5. Spoon the batter into the prepared tins.

6. Bake until the tops of the cupcakes are lightly browned and springy when lightly touched with a fingertip, 18 to 20 minutes. Cool completely in the tins on a wire rack before frosting.

7. To make the frosting, combine the sugar, water, egg white, cream of tartar, and salt in the top of a double boiler. Place over simmering water and beat with an electric mixer on high speed until stiff peaks form.

8. Remove from the heat; add the orange zest, orange extract, and food colorings. Beat with the electric mixer on high speed until well blended.

Note: Both the cupcakes and the frosting are intensely flavored with orange. If you prefer a subtler taste, cut the quantities of orange zest and extract in both of the recipes in half.

DEVIL-IN-DISGUISE CUPCAKES

Masquerading as devil's food, these egg-free cupcakes weigh in at less than 5 grams of fat apiece—with no cholesterol. Topped with swirls of Billowy Frosting, or served "à la mode" with tiny scoops of frozen yogurt, they're surprisingly satisfying. This is a variation of a recipe created by the Hershey's Cocoa kitchens.

Makes 12 cupcakes

1¼ cups all-purpose flour
⅓ cup unsweetened cocoa powder
½ teaspoon baking powder
½ teaspoon baking soda
Large pinch salt

⅓ cup light corn-oil spread
⅔ cup sugar
1 cup low-fat buttermilk
1 teaspoon pure vanilla extract

1. Preheat the oven to 350 degrees. Line 12 muffin tins with paper liners or spray the tins with vegetable cooking spray and flour them. Set aside.

2. In a small bowl, whisk together the flour, cocoa, baking powder, baking soda, and salt; set aside.

3. In a medium saucepan over moderate heat, melt the corn oil spread; remove from the heat and stir in the sugar until well blended. Beat in the buttermilk, then the vanilla.

4. Pour the buttermilk mixture over the dry ingredients in the bowl; beat until smooth with a wire whisk, then with a heavy spoon. The batter will resemble chocolate pudding.

5. Spoon the batter into the prepared tins.

6. Bake until the cupcakes are cracked on top and springy when gently pressed with a fingertip, about 20 minutes. Cool in the tins on a wire rack for 10 minutes. Carefully remove from the tins to the wire rack and cool completely.

Frostings, Glazes, Sauces, and Fillings

F or many cupcake lovers, the cupcake is just a convenient vehicle for the frosting, be it a deep dark fudge frosting or a creamy vanilla buttercream. Those with simpler tastes often opt for a glaze instead. Although most of the cupcake recipes suggest appropriate frostings or glazes, you'll undoubtedly come up with your own favorite combinations.

Fillings add yet another vehicle for flavor, whether they're spread between the layers of a split cupcake or piped into the center of the cupcake through the bottom, using a pastry bag fitted with a sharp round tip.

Sauces turn cupcakes into elegant plate-and-fork affairs, lovely as an after-dinner dessert.

MAPLE WHIPPED CREAM

Sprinkle cupcakes topped with this café au lait–colored cream with minced and cooled toasted walnuts.

Makes about 2 cups, enough for 12 cupcakes

1 cup heavy or whipping cream, chilled

¼ cup maple syrup
1 teaspoon maple flavoring

In a small deep bowl, combine the cream, maple syrup, and maple flavoring. Beat with an electric mixer on high speed until the mixture forms stiff, spreadable peaks.

Vanilla whipped cream

Stabilizing the cream with gelatin keeps it fluffy longer, although it should only be placed on the cupcakes shortly before serving time. Place the cream in the refrigerator and rewhip it a bit just before piping or spreading it onto the cupcakes. The cream may be varied with the addition of grated orange zest, crushed peanut brittle, toasted coconut, or other flavorings.

Makes about 2 cups, enough for 12 cupcakes

½ teaspoon unflavored gelatin
1½ teaspoons water
1 cup heavy or whipping cream, chilled

3 tablespoons confectioners' sugar, sifted if lumpy
1 teaspoon pure vanilla extract

1. In a small heatproof bowl or cup, sprinkle the gelatin over the water; let stand a minute or two to soften.

2. Place the bowl or cup in a skillet filled with hot, not boiling, water. Heat, stirring, until the gelatin dissolves. Remove from the heat.

3. In a small deep bowl with an electric mixer on high speed, beat the cream, sugar, and vanilla until soft peaks form. Beat in the dissolved gelatin. Continue beating until the mixture forms stiff peaks.

4. If desired, spoon the whipped cream into a pastry bag fitted with a star tip. Decorate the tops of cooled cupcakes with swirls of whipped cream. Keep refrigerated until serving time.

SQUIGGLE FROSTING

Just the right consistency to add the familiar white curlicues down the middle of chocolate cupcakes enrobed in Chocolate Satin Glaze. Or, tint and use to make the "seams" of baseball cupcakes.

Makes about ½ cup, enough to decorate 12 cupcakes

⅔ cup confectioners' sugar, sifted if lumpy

1 to 2 tablespoons milk

In a small bowl, combine the sugar and 1 tablespoon of the milk until smooth, adding enough of the remaining milk, drop by drop, to make a thick, smooth frosting that can be piped through a pastry bag fitted with a small plain tip.

HAZELNUT CREAM

This mousselike topping is intensely nutty, owing to the use of sweetened hazelnut paste, available in specialty food shops or by mail through Dean & Deluca, 560 Broadway, New York, NY 10012 (212-431-1691).

Makes about 2 cups, enough for 12 cupcakes

¾ cup heavy or whipping cream (see Note)

½ cup sweetened hazelnut paste

1. In a small bowl with an electric mixer on high speed, beat the cream until it is stiff.

2. In another small bowl, stir about ¼ cup of the whipped cream into the hazelnut paste, to lighten it. Then fold in the remaining whipped cream.

3. Use the cream as a cupcake filling (it's especially luscious placed over a dab of melted chocolate) or frosting. Or, pipe it into rosettes through a pastry bag, using a star tip, then top each rosette with a perfect hazelnut. Another time, spread a smooth layer of the

cream atop completely cooled cupcakes. Freeze until firm, then cover with Bittersweet Ganache. The cream can be refrigerated for several hours before it's used. Once it's used on cupcakes, they should be refrigerated, too.

Note: For a lighter, less sweet topping, increase the cream to 1 cup.

DOUBLE CHIP FROSTING

This frosting firms up when chilled, so it should be spread on the cupcakes right after it's made, while it's still soft. Otherwise, let it come back to room temperature before using it. It's very adaptable, too: To impart additional flavor nuances, add grated orange zest, chopped nuts, or peppermint extract.

Makes about 1½ cups, enough for 12 cupcakes

1½ cups miniature semisweet chocolate pieces
¼ cup heavy or whipping cream
½ cup (1 stick) unsalted butter

½ cup sifted confectioners' sugar
1 teaspoon pure vanilla extract
½ teaspoon chocolate extract
  (optional)

1. In a medium-size heavy saucepan, combine 1 cup of the chocolate pieces with the cream and butter. Cook over moderate heat, stirring often, until the mixture is smooth and the chocolate is completely melted. Remove from the heat.

2. With a heavy spoon or wire whisk, beat in the sugar, vanilla extract, and chocolate extract.

3. Set the saucepan inside a large bowl filled with ice. Beat with an electric mixer on high speed until the frosting is cold and holds its shape. Do not overbeat. (If you do, and the frosting gets too firm, simply reheat it until it softens, then gently beat it again.)

4. Fold in the remaining ½ cup chocolate pieces, or frost the cupcakes, then sprinkle the tops with the chocolate pieces chill the frosted cupcakes.

Vanilla and Cinnamon Butter-Creams

The cinnamon version is both spicy and an attractive tan color.

Makes about 2 cups, enough for 2 dozen cupcakes

¾ cup (1½ sticks) unsalted butter, softened
2⅓ to 2½ cups sifted confectioners' sugar

¼ cup sour cream
1 tablespoon pure vanilla extract
⅛ teaspoon salt
2 teaspoons ground cinnamon

1. In a large bowl with an electric mixer on medium speed, combine the butter, sugar, sour cream, vanilla, and salt until light and well blended.

2. Transfer half of the buttercream to a small bowl; beat in the cinnamon.

CITRUS AND COFFEE– RUM BUTTERCREAMS

Here's another two-way recipe.

Makes about 2½ cups, enough for 2 dozen cupcakes

1¼ cups (2½ sticks) unsalted butter, softened
3 cups sifted confectioners' sugar
¼ cup sour cream
⅛ teaspoon salt
2 teaspoons grated orange and/or lemon zest
1½ teaspoons fresh orange and/or lemon juice
1 tablespoon instant espresso powder
1½ teaspoons light or dark rum

1. In a large bowl with an electric mixer on medium speed, combine the butter, sugar, sour cream, and salt until light and well blended.

2. Transfer half of the buttercream to a small bowl. To one half of the buttercream, beat in the orange and/or lemon zest and juice until blended.

3. Dissolve the espresso powder in the rum in a cup. Beat this mixture into the remaining buttercream until well blended.

CHOCOLATE-PEANUT BUTTER FROSTING

Wickedly rich, a frosting for those with candy-loving palates. If it doesn't seem like overkill, spread this on chocolate cupcakes. Otherwise, use it atop any vanilla-flavored ones.

Makes about 1⅓ cups, enough for 12 cupcakes

½ cup creamy peanut butter
2 tablespoons (¼ stick) unsalted butter, softened
Large pinch salt
1 teaspoon pure vanilla extract

3 to 4 tablespoons milk
1½ cups confectioners' sugar, sifted if lumpy
¼ cup unsweetened cocoa powder, sifted if lumpy

1. In a medium bowl with an electric mixer on high speed, beat together the peanut butter, butter, and salt until well blended.

2. Beat in the vanilla and 3 tablespoons of the milk until well blended.

3. Gradually beat in the sugar and cocoa, adding more milk, if necessary, to achieve a smooth, spreadable consistency.

Sour cream–fudge frosting

Just two ingredients go into this luxurious frosting. It firms up when it's refrigerated but will get soft again if it's left at room temperature.

Makes about 2 cups, enough for 12 cupcakes

2 cups (12 ounces) semisweet chocolate pieces OR 4 bars (3 ounces each)

semisweet chocolate, chopped
1 cup sour cream or plain yogurt

1. In a medium heavy saucepan over very low heat, or in the top of a double boiler over simmering water, melt the chocolate. Remove from the heat.

2. Stir in the sour cream until smooth and well blended. The mixture will be very soft. Chill it, if necessary, until it is of spreading consistency. Refrigerate the frosted cupcakes.

VARIATION

Instead of plain yogurt, substitute a fruit-flavored variety such as raspberry or apricot; add 1 teaspoon of fruit-flavored liqueur along with the yogurt.

CHOCOLATE–CREAM CHEESE FROSTING

This frosting is dense and satisfying, with a candylike quality. Use 1 ounce of chocolate for a sweet flavor that kids will like; use 2 ounces for a more intense, grown-up taste.

Makes about ¾ cup, enough for 12 cupcakes

4 ounces cream cheese, softened
2 tablespoons (¼ stick) unsalted butter, softened
1 cup confectioners' sugar, sifted if lumpy

½ teaspoon pure vanilla extract
1 to 2 squares (1 ounce each) unsweetened chocolate, melted

In a small bowl with a large heavy spoon, beat together the cream cheese and butter until smooth and well blended. Beat in the sugar and vanilla, then the chocolate. Refrigerate the frosting until it is of spreading consistency. The frosting can be made ahead and refrigerated; remove it from the refrigerator about 30 minutes before using it, to let it soften a bit.

COCONUTTY VANILLA–CHIP FROSTING

This vanilla buttercream gets its crunch from shreds of coconut, toasted almonds, and chocolate chips. It's wonderful on Devil's Food Cupcakes.

Makes about 2 cups, enough for 12 cupcakes generously

¼ cups slivered almonds
½ cup (1 stick) unsalted butter, softened
3 cups sifted confectioners' sugar

1 teaspoon pure vanilla extract
¼ teaspoon pure almond extract
½ cup semisweet chocolate pieces
¼ cup sweetened flaked coconut

1. Preheat the oven to 350 degrees. Place the almonds in a single layer in a pie plate. Bake until golden, 5 to 10 minutes. Remove from the oven; let cool completely.

2. In a medium bowl with an electric mixer on high speed, beat the butter until it is creamy and smooth. Slowly beat in the sugar, about a cup at a time, beating well after each addition, then beat in the vanilla and almond extracts.

3. Beat in the chocolate pieces, coconut, and toasted almonds. Continue beating for 1 minute longer, to break up the nuts and chips.

Peanut butter
Frosting

A little of this super-rich frosting goes a long way. Try it on peanut butter or chocolate cupcakes. For a more elaborate presentation, re-frigerate or freeze the frosted cupcakes, then glaze the tops with Bittersweet Ganache.

Makes about 1⅓ cups, enough for 12 cupcakes

½ cup creamy peanut butter
¼ cup (1/2 stick) unsalted butter, softened
2 ounces cream cheese, softened

1 teaspoon pure vanilla extract
1 cup confectioners' sugar, sifted if
  lumpy

1. In a small bowl, combine the peanut butter, butter, and cream cheese with a heavy spoon until smooth and well blended. Beat in the vanilla.

2. Beat in the sugar, a little at a time, until smooth.

CREAM CHEESE FROSTING

This makes a generous amount of frosting—enough to top a dozen cupcakes lavishly or give two dozen cupcakes a nice "schmear." Because it has less confectioners' sugar than the average cream cheese frosting, it's quite soft until it's chilled.

Makes about 1¾ cups, enough for 12 to 24 cupcakes (see paragraph above)

½ cup (1 stick) unsalted butter, softened
1 package (8 ounces) cream cheese, softened

1½ teaspoons grated lemon zest
1½ teaspoons grated orange zest
Pinch salt
1 cup confectioners' sugar, sifted if

1. In a medium bowl, beat together the butter and cream cheese with an electric mixer on high speed until very light and well blended. Beat in the lemon and orange zests and the salt.

2. Lower the mixer speed to low. Beat in the sugar until well blended. The frosting will be very soft. If desired, refrigerate it for about 15 minutes for easier spreading. To pre-

vent the frosting from running off the tops of the cupcakes, refrigerate them once they've been frosted.

ROCKY ROAD FROSTING

Milk chocolate, miniature marshmallows, and pecans or walnuts create a confectionlike topping.

Makes about 3 cups, enough to top 12 cupcakes
lavishly—with leftovers for nibbling!

1¾ cups milk-chocolate pieces
1 square (1 ounce) unsweetened
  chocolate, chopped
½ cup (1 stick) unsalted butter,
  softened

1 teaspoon pure vanilla extract
Pinch salt
1 cup miniature marshmallows
¾ cup finely chopped pecans or
  walnuts

1. In a medium heavy saucepan over low heat, melt 1 cup of the milk-chocolate pieces with the unsweetened chocolate, or melt in the microwave (see page 22). Remove from the heat.

2. Add the butter, vanilla, and salt to the melted chocolate and stir until the butter melts and is incorporated into the chocolate. Let stand until the chocolate is at room temperature. (The mixture can be left overnight, covered.)

3. Use a hand-held mixer, or transfer the chocolate to the bowl of a standing mixer. Whip the chocolate at high speed until it holds soft peaks.

4. Fold in the reserved chocolate pieces, marshmallows, and nuts.

DRIED-CRANBERRY WHIP

My friend Jessica Feinleib created this vibrantly colored topping as a nonfat alternative to frosting. Try it on No-Cholesterol Pumpkin Cupcakes or Feather-Light Orange Cupcakes—just a tablespoon is enough for each cupcake.

Makes about 1 cup, enough for 12 cupcakes

1/2 cup firmly packed light brown sugar
1/2 cup water

1 cup dried cranberries
A few drops maple flavoring or pure vanilla extract (optional)

1. In a small saucepan, combine the sugar and water. Bring to a boil over moderate heat. Lower the heat and simmer until the sugar is completely dissolved.

2. Add the dried cranberries, stirring them into the syrup so they are completely immersed. Remove from the heat. Let the mixture stand until it reaches room temperature. Add the maple flavoring, if desired. (I prefer the topping without extra flavoring; it retains a more pronounced cranberry flavor and color.)

3. Place the syrup and cranberries in the container of a blender or food processor. Cover and process until blended and thickened. Transfer to a small bowl. Refrigerate any left-over topping and use on toast, waffles, pancakes, or hot cereal.

BILLOWY FROSTING

This is the classic seven-minute frosting (because only one egg white is used, it actually takes about four to six minutes to beat), a very sweet meringue topping that swirls to perfection. Silky texture and dramatic appearance give the frosting a rich effect, even though it's fat free.

Makes about 1⅓ cups, enough for 12 cupcakes

1 egg white
⅔ cup granulated sugar
2 tablespoons cold water

1 teaspoon light corn syrup
⅛ teaspoon cream of tartar
½ teaspoon pure vanilla extract

1. In the top of a double boiler or in a heatproof bowl that will fit snugly on top of a saucepan, combine the egg white, sugar, water, corn syrup, and cream of tartar. Place over, not in, boiling water and beat with a hand-held electric mixer on high speed until the mixture forms very soft shiny peaks, 4 to 7 minutes. (This can also be done by hand with a whisk; you'll have to double the beating time.)

2. Remove the pan from the heat and add the vanilla. Continue beating for another

minute or two, until the frosting thickens slightly. Immediately top cupcakes with the frosting, making decorative swirls, then quickly add garnishes. As the frosting stands, it will set on the outside but will remain quite soft on the inside.

Note: Since the frosting is based on egg white, it should not be prepared more than 6 hours before serving time, or it may start to separate.

VARIATIONS

Peppermint: Omit the vanilla and substitute ½ teaspoon peppermint extract and 2 tablespoons crushed peppermint candy. If desired, tint the frosting pale pink with red food coloring.

Citrus: Substitute 1 tablespoon lemon juice for 1 tablespoon of the water. Omit the vanilla and substitute 1/2 teaspoon orange or lemon extract and ½ to 1 teaspoon grated lemon or orange zest. If desired, tint the frosting pale yellow or orange with food coloring.

Coffee-Toffee: Replace the 2 tablespoons cold water with homemade coffee concentrate: Combine 1½ teaspoons instant espresso powder with 1 tablespoon hot water until dissolved; add 1 tablespoon of cold water and let cool completely. Add 1/4 cup crushed toffee or coffee candy along with the vanilla.

Pastel: Tint the frosting with a few drops of liquid food coloring when you add the vanilla.

Coconut: Add ½ teaspoon coconut extract and ⅓ cup sweetened shredded coconut along with the vanilla.

Raspberry: Replace the water with 2 tablespoons of sieved puréed fresh or frozen and thawed raspberries. Replace the vanilla with 1 teaspoon raspberry brandy or liqueur.

Butterscotch-Rum: Replace the granulated sugar with firmly packed dark brown sugar. Add ¼ teaspoon rum extract along with the vanilla.

Maple-Walnut: Replace the granulated sugar with maple sugar. Add ¼ teaspoon maple extract and ¼ cup finely chopped toasted walnuts along with the vanilla.

HARD-SAUCE FROSTING

Just a little of this ultra-rich frosting goes a long way! Spread it thinly over Rum-Raisin Cupcakes for a taste reminiscent of plum pudding.

Makes a scant 1 cup, enough for 12 cupcakes

¼ cup (½ stick) unsalted butter,
  softened
1½ cups confectioners' sugar, sifted
  if lumpy

1 tablespoon very hot water
1 tablespoon rum
½ teaspoon rum extract
Pinch salt

1. In a small bowl, beat the butter until it is soft and creamy with an electric mixer on high speed. Lower the mixer speed to low. Gradually add the sugar, beating until well blended.

2. Add the water and the rum, a bit at a time, until well incorporated, then the rum extract and the salt. The consistency will be somewhere between that of a glaze and a frosting; it will firm up with standing.

A BIG BATCH OF BUTTERCREAM

This versatile frosting is enough for twenty-four cupcakes. For a party, I like to divide the frosting into smaller batches and flavor and tint each one differently. That way, even if I've baked only one type of cupcake, the party platter will still appear bountiful.

Makes about 2⅓ cups, enough for 2 dozen cupcakes

½ cup (1 stick) unsalted butter, softened

1 box (1 pound) confectioners' sugar, sifted if lumpy

¼ to ⅓ cup milk or heavy cream

1 tablespoon pure vanilla extract

¼ teaspoon salt

1. In a medium bowl, beat the butter with an electric mixer on high speed until it is light and fluffy. Gradually beat in the sugar, alternately with ¼ cup of the milk or cream, beating well after each addition.

2. Beat in the vanilla and the salt until well incorporated. Add more milk or cream, if necessary, to produce a nice spreading texture.

VARIATIONS

The following variations are for a whole batch of buttercream. If desired, the buttercream can be divided into smaller amounts and the flavorings can be reduced accordingly.

Maple-Walnut Buttercream: Substitute maple syrup for half of the milk or cream. Reduce the vanilla to 1 teaspoon and add 1 teaspoon maple flavoring. When the frosting is of the right consistency, beat in ½ cup toasted and cooled minced walnuts.

Coffee Buttercream: Reduce the vanilla to 1 teaspoon. Dissolve 1 tablespoon instant espresso powder in 2 teaspoons of hot water; cool, then add to the buttercream.

Chocolate Buttercream: Add 3 squares (1 ounce each) of unsweetened chocolate, melted and cooled, to the creamed butter.

Orange Buttercream: Replace the milk or cream with fresh orange juice. Replace the vanilla with 1 tablespoon grated orange zest and 1/4 teaspoon orange extract. Tint the frosting a delicate orange with food coloring, if desired.

Lemon Buttercream: Replace the milk or cream with fresh lemon juice. Replace the vanilla with 1 tablespoon grated lemon zest and 1/4 teaspoon lemon extract. Tint the frosting a delicate yellow with food coloring, if desired.

Almond-Amaretto Buttercream: Reduce the vanilla to 1 teaspoon. Add 1 tablespoon amaretto liqueur and 1/4 teaspoon pure almond extract.

Pecan-Bourbon Buttercream: Reduce the vanilla to 1 teaspoon. Add 1 tablespoon bour-

bon. When the frosting is of the right consistency, beat in ½ cup toasted and cooled minced pecans.

Pineapple Buttercream: Replace the vanilla with 1 tablespoon fresh lemon juice. When the frosting is of the right consistency, beat in ⅔ cup drained crushed pineapple.

Tangy Sour-Cream Buttercream: Substitute sour cream for the milk or cream. Add a large pinch of cinnamon and/or nutmeg along with the salt, if desired.

Chocolate-Orange Buttercream: Add 3 squares (1 ounce each) unsweetened chocolate, melted and cooled, to the creamed butter. Reduce the vanilla to 1 teaspoon and add 1 tablespoon Grand Marnier or other orange liqueur and 1 tablespoon grated orange zest.

Rum-Raisin Buttercream: In a small bowl, combine ½ cup raisins and 3 tablespoons rum. Cover and let stand for at least 4 hours. (The mixture may be left for up to a week; in fact, the raisins will get plump and fragrant with longer standing.) Drain the raisins, reserving any rum that has not been absorbed. Pulse-chop the raisins in a food processor or blender; set aside. Reduce the vanilla to 1 teaspoon; add the reserved rum and ½ teaspoon rum extract, if desired. When the frosting is of the right consistency, beat in the chopped raisins.

Dried-Cherry Buttercream: In a small saucepan, combine ½ cup dried cherries and water to cover. Bring to a simmer over moderate heat. Drain the cherries; chop them coarsely; set aside. Reduce the vanilla to 1 teaspoon. Add 1 tablespoon brandy or rum. When the frosting is of the right consistency, beat in the chopped cherries. Tint the frosting a delicate pink with food coloring, if desired.

Peppermint-Stick Buttercream: Replace the vanilla with 1½ teaspoons peppermint extract and 1 tablespoon white or green crème de menthe, if desired. When the frosting is of the right consistency, beat in ½ cup finely crushed peppermint candy. Tint the frosting a delicate pink or green with food coloring, if desired.

BROWNED BUTTER FROSTING

A very sweet frosting with an intense butter flavor and nut-brown color, best used to top less-rich cupcakes such as Oatmeal–Dried Cherry and Prune-Walnut. If desired, add ⅓ cup finely chopped toasted nuts.

Makes about 1½ cups, enough for 12 cupcakes

¾ cup (1½ sticks) unsalted butter, softened

4 cups confectioners' sugar, sifted if lumpy

⅛ teaspoon salt

¼ cup hot milk

4 teaspoons pure vanilla extract

1. In a small saucepan over moderately low heat, melt ½ cup (1 stick) of the butter; continue heating, swirling the pan to prevent burning, until the butter turns nut brown. Pour into a medium bowl.

2. With a heavy wire whisk or electric mixer on low speed, beat in the confectioners'

sugar and salt alternately with the milk and vanilla extract, until the frosting is smooth. Beat in the remaining butter, bit by bit.

3. Refrigerate the frosting until it cools and thickens enough to spread. Keep frosted cupcakes refrigerated, since the frosting may run off if it gets too soft.

CAFÉ BRÛLOT BUTTER-CREAM

This sultry frosting has all the flavors of the flaming coffee drink for which it's named—orange, cinnamon, and cardamom. The instant espresso powder blends right into the buttercream, so there's no need to dissolve it ahead of time.

Makes about 1⅔ cups, enough to frost 12 cupcakes generously

¾ cup (1½ sticks) unsalted butter, softened
1¾ cups sifted confectioners' sugar
2 teaspoons instant espresso powder
2 teaspoons Kahlúa, orange liqueur, or brandy
1 teaspoon grated orange zest
½ teaspoon ground cinnamon
¼ teaspoon ground cardamom
¼ teaspoon pure vanilla extract

1. In a small bowl, beat the butter until light with an electric mixer on high speed.

2. Gradually beat in the sugar, then the espresso powder, liqueur, orange zest, cinnamon, cardamom, and vanilla. Continue beating until the mixture is well blended and fluffy.

Mocha buttercream

A spiritually compatible topping for Mocha Cupcakes. Left at room temperature, it resembles a mousse, which makes it more suitable as a filling. Refrigerated, it firms up to a frosting consistency.

Makes about 2 cups, enough for 12 to 24 cupcakes (see paragraph above)

1 bar (3 ounces) bittersweet chocolate, chopped, or ½ cup (3 ounces) semisweet chocolate pieces
½ cup (1 stick) unsalted butter
2 cups confectioners' sugar, sifted if lumpy
½ cup unsweetened cocoa powder
Pinch salt

⅓ cup milk
2 tablespoons Kahlúa or other coffee liqueur
1 tablespoon instant espresso powder, dissolved in 1 teaspoon hot water
1 teaspoon pure vanilla extract

1. In a small heavy saucepan, combine the chocolate with 3 tablespoons of the butter. Melt over low heat, stirring occasionally.

2. In a medium bowl, combine the sugar, cocoa, salt, milk, Kahlúa, dissolved espresso powder, and vanilla. Beat with an electric mixer on medium speed until blended.

3. Beat in the melted chocolate mixture, then the remaining 5 tablespoons of butter, bit by bit, until blended and fluffy. Use the mixture at room temperature as a filling. Or, chill it until it achieves the right consistency for spreading.

TOASTED COCONUT CREAM

This not-too-sweet combination can be used as a topping for cupcakes (it looks especially striking on chocolate cupcakes), or dolloped alongside them on the serving plate. Toasting the coconut adds both flavor and crunch.

Makes about 1½ cups, enough for 12 cupcakes

1 tablespoon unsalted butter
1 cup sweetened flaked coconut
½ cup heavy or whipping cream,
  chilled

3 tablespoons sour cream
3 tablespoons confectioners' sugar
1½ teaspoons pure vanilla extract

1. In a large skillet over moderately high heat, melt the butter; sauté the coconut in the butter, stirring often, until it turns golden brown. Watch for burning! Remove from the heat. Transfer the coconut to a plate lined with paper towels. Set aside.

2. In a small chilled bowl, combine the heavy cream and the sour cream. Beat with an electric mixer on high speed until the mixture begins to thicken.

3. Add the confectioners' sugar and vanilla and continue beating until the mixture forms soft or firm peaks, depending on whether you'll be using it as an accompaniment or a topping. Fold in 1/2 cup of the coconut.

4. Use the cream as a topping or an accompaniment, sprinkling the remaining 1/2 cup coconut on top just before serving, to preserve its crunchiness.

WHITE-CHOCOLATE FROSTING

Though white chocolate is not really chocolate at all, it shares chocolate's satisfying texture, as evidenced in this simple recipe. Because this frosting is rich, it won't produce a lavish mantle on the cupcakes. If you want a more generous covering, double the quantities.

Makes about 1 cup, enough for 12 cupcakes

¼ cup heavy or whipping cream
1 cup white-chocolate pieces

2 tablespoons (¼ stick) unsalted butter

1. In a small heavy saucepan, heat the cream just until it starts to simmer.

2. Add the white-chocolate pieces, shaking the pan to immerse them in the cream, then

add the butter. Let the mixture stand for 1 minute, then beat with a wire whisk until the chocolate pieces and butter dissolve and the mixture is smooth.

3. Refrigerate the mixture until cold, then whip it with a wire whisk until fluffy. Spread on completely cooled cupcakes. Refrigerate the cupcakes, if desired, to firm up the frosting. (Otherwise it will be quite soft.)

WHIPPED MILK-
CHOCOLATE FROSTING

Dark chocolate isn't for everyone. Here's a creamy frosting based on only two ingredients that will suit those with lighter chocolate tastes just fine.

Makes about 1⅓ cups, enough for 12 cupcakes

½ cup heavy or whipping cream
1 cup milk chocolate pieces or 2 bars

(3 ounces each) milk chocolate,
broken into small pieces

1. Pour the cream into a small heavy saucepan; place over moderately high heat until the cream begins to boil. Remove from the heat.

2. Add the chocolate pieces to the hot cream, shaking the pan so all of the chocolate is immersed in the cream. Let the mixture stand for 1 minute, or until the chocolate is melted.

3. Beat the melted chocolate and cream with a large heavy spoon until the mixture is smooth and well blended. Transfer to a small bowl. Let cool to room temperature.

4. Whip the chocolate mixture with an electric mixer on high speed until it thickens and forms soft peaks. Dip the tops of cupcakes, one at a time, into the frosting, swirling to make attractive peaks. The frosting will still be soft but will thicken upon standing.

Note: The cream can be heated in a 2-cup glass measure in the microwave. Cook on high for 1 minute and 20 seconds, then proceed with the rest of the recipe.

LEMON CURD

A sweet-tart combination that can be used as a filling or topping, either alone or folded into whipped cream, as described below. Either way, It's a natural with carrot, zucchini, or ginger cupcakes.

Makes about 1 cup, enough for 12 cupcakes

4 egg yolks
¾ cup sugar
⅓ cup fresh lemon juice

¼ cup (½ stick) unsalted butter, cut up
1½ teaspoons grated lemon zest

1. In a heavy saucepan, whisk together the egg yolks and sugar; gradually whisk in the lemon juice, then throw in the butter pieces.

2. Cook over moderately low heat, whisking constantly, until the mixture is on the verge of boiling—*but do not allow it to boil.* Immediately remove from the heat.

3. Strain the mixture through a fine sieve into a small bowl. Stir in the lemon zest. Let

cool to room temperature, then cover the surface directly with plastic wrap and refrigerate until completely cold.

VARIATION

Lemon Curd Cream: Whip ½ cup heavy or whipping cream until stiff. Stir a bit of the cream into ½ cup cold lemon curd, to lighten it, then fold in the remainder. Refrigerate until the mixture firms up. The cream will never be very firm, so it's best used as a filling, or added to the tops of cupcakes just before serving. (If you want to complete the cupcakes an hour or so ahead, be sure to refrigerate them once you've topped them with the cream.) It can also be served alongside cupcakes for a more elegant presentation. (Makes about 1⅓ cups.)

Cocoa Frosting

This frosting's luxurious flavor and texture belie its quick preparation.

Makes about 1⅓ cups, enough for 12 cupcakes amply

2 cups unsifted confectioners' sugar
⅔ cup unsweetened cocoa powder
Large pinch salt
¼ cup milk

½ teaspoon pure vanilla extract
¼ cup (½ stick) unsalted butter,
  softened

1. In a small bowl, combine the sugar, cocoa, and salt until blended.

2. Add the milk and vanilla; beat until smooth with a hand mixer or a large heavy spoon.

3. Beat in the butter until the frosting is of spreading consistency.

CHOCOLATE–RASPBERRY GLAZE/FROSTING

Chocolate and fruit flavors go so well together! This frosting glorifies my favorite combination. It can be poured as a glaze or cooled and whipped to frosting consistency. Either way, it freezes and thaws well.

Makes about 1 cup (more if whipped), enough for 12 cupcakes

⅓ cup heavy or whipping cream
1 cup (6 ounces) semisweet chocolate pieces OR 2 bars (3 ounces each) semisweet or bittersweet chocolate, chopped fine

¼ cup raspberry preserves
2 tablespoons unsalted butter

1. In a small heavy saucepan over moderate heat, bring the cream to a simmer; remove from the heat.

2. Add the chocolate, preserves, and butter, shaking the pan to immerse the chocolate

and as much of the preserves and butter as possible. Let stand for 1½ minutes, or until the chocolate has melted.

3. Beat the mixture with a wire whisk until it is smooth. Cool until thick enough to use as a glaze. Or cool completely and whip to spreading consistency.

BUTTERSCOTCH GLAZE/FROSTING

This recipe produces either a lustrous glaze or a silky-smooth frosting. Its orange hue makes it a natural for Halloween cupcakes!

Makes about ⅔ cup, enough for 12 cupcakes

⅓ cup heavy or whipping cream   1 cup butterscotch pieces

1. In a small heavy saucepan, heat the cream just until it starts to simmer.

2. Add the butterscotch pieces, shaking the pan to immerse them in the cream. Let the mixture stand for 1 minute, then beat it with a wire whisk until the butterscotch pieces dissolve and the mixture is smooth.

3. Bring the mixture to room temperature and use it as a glaze; the cupcakes may require two coatings. Or refrigerate it until it's good and cold, then whip it with a wire whisk just until fluffy; don't overwhip or the frosting may curdle. Spread on completely cooled

SNOWY-WHITE GLAZE

This all-purpose glaze can be left pristine white, or tinted and flavored to suit the occasion. Smooth it over the tops of cupcakes, or let it thicken slightly with standing, then drizzle it in dramatic zigzags or swirls.

Makes about 1 cup, enough for 12 cupcakes

1⅓ cups confectioners' sugar, sifted if lumpy

2 tablespoons milk

In a small bowl, vigorously beat the sugar and milk with a spoon until smooth. If desired, tint the frosting with food coloring and/or add a few drops of your favorite extract. Let stand until the glaze is thick enough to coat the tops of the cupcakes. If you wish to make decorations that will hold their shape, let the glaze stand until it thickens a bit more.

VARIATIONS

Lemon Glaze: Replace the milk with the juice and grated zest of 1 lemon.

Orange Glaze: Replace the milk with the grated zest of 1 orange and 2 tablespoons of orange juice.

Almond Glaze: Add ⅛ teaspoon almond extract to the glaze.

Cinnamon Glaze: Add ½ teaspoon ground cinnamon to the glaze.

Coffee Glaze: Substitute 1 tablespoon cold, double-strength brewed coffee and 1 tablespoon Kahlúa for the milk.

BLACK-AND-WHITE GLAZE

This two-tone glaze can be used two ways! Decorate half a batch of cupcakes with the white glaze, the other with the chocolate. Or use it to make "black and whites," cupcake versions of the jumbo harlequin cookies, by dipping half of each cupcake top in the white glaze, then dipping the other half in the chocolate glaze. For a more colorful effect, tint the white icing with liquid food coloring.

Makes about 1½ cups, enough for 12 cupcakes

4 cups confectioners' sugar, sifted if
  lumpy
¼ cup light corn syrup

¼ cup water
1 square (1 ounce) unsweetened
  chocolate, chopped

1. In the top of a double boiler, combine the sugar, corn syrup, and water. Place over simmering, not boiling, water and heat, stirring often, until the sugar dissolves and the mixture is well blended. Remove about half of the icing to a small bowl.

2. Add the chopped chocolate to the remaining icing in the pan. Return to the simmering water and heat, stirring often, until the chocolate melts. If the icing gets too thick, add a bit of warm water, drop by drop, until a spreadable consistency is achieved.

Note: To retain the glaze's gloss, always keep the water in the double boiler at a simmer, never a boil. When making "black and whites," let one half of the cupcake's glaze harden a bit before dipping cupcake in the second glaze.

CREAM CHEESE GLAZE

A lighter, less sweet topping for Carrot Cupcakes than the traditional Cream Cheese Frosting.

Makes about 1 ⅓ cups, enough for 12 cupcakes

1 package (8 ounces) cream cheese, softened

1 ½ cups confectioners' sugar, or more as needed, sifted if lumpy

¼ cup fresh orange juice, or more as needed

1 tablespoon grated orange zest (optional)

In a small bowl with an electric mixer on medium speed, beat the cream cheese until it is very light. Gradually beat in the sugar, then the orange juice, until the mixture forms a thick glaze. Add more orange juice or sugar, if necessary, to adjust the consistency. Beat in the orange zest.

APRICOT GLAZE

For a nice surprise, brush this tangy glaze over cupcakes before they're frosted or topped with a layer of marzipan.

Makes about ½ cup, enough for 12 cupcakes

1 cup apricot preserves

1. Place the preserves in a small heavy saucepan. Cook over moderately high heat, stirring often, until the preserves melt and start to boil. Lower the heat slightly. Let simmer for a few minutes, until the mixture thickens somewhat.

2. Remove the saucepan from the heat. Strain the preserves through a fine sieve. Cool slightly, then brush onto cupcakes. Transfer any unused glaze to a glass jar and refrigerate. Reheat the glaze to use it again.

BITTERSWEET GANACHE

The classic chocolate glaze made from only bittersweet chocolate and heavy cream. Use it to top plain cupcakes or those that have been filled or frosted and thoroughly chilled.

Makes about 2 cups, enough for 12 cupcakes

½ pound bittersweet or semisweet chocolate, chopped

1 cup heavy or whipping cream

1. Place the chocolate in a medium bowl; set aside.

2. In a medium heavy saucepan, bring the cream to a boil over moderate heat; remove from the heat.

3. Pour the cream over the chocolate, shaking the bowl to immerse the chocolate completely. Let stand for about 1½ minutes, or until the chocolate has melted.

4. Gently beat the mixture with a wire whisk until it is smooth.

5. Let the mixture cool to room temperature. It will be thick enough to use as a glaze.

6. Place the cupcakes to be glazed on a wire rack over an aluminum foil–lined cookie sheet. Slowly pour the glaze over the cupcakes.

ESPRESSO GLAZE

Speckled with espresso powder, this lustrous glaze is equally delicious on Espresso-Chocolate Chip Cupcakes or any chocolate cupcakes. Use the full tablespoon of espresso powder if you like a robust coffee flavor; otherwise, 2 teaspoons is sufficient.

Makes about ¾ cup, enough to top 12 cupcakes lightly (see Note 2)

1 cup sifted confectioners' sugar
2 tablespoons (¼ stick) unsalted
  butter, softened
2 teaspoons to 1 tablespoon instant
  espresso powder

1 tablespoon Kahlúa or other coffee-
  flavored liqueur
1 tablespoon milk

1. In a small bowl with a large heavy spoon, beat together the sugar, butter, and espresso powder until blended.

2. Stir in the Kahlúa and milk and beat until smooth, switching to a wire whisk if any lumps form. Let stand for a few minutes before spooning onto the top center of each cupcake. Let stand until set.

Note 1: For a more elegant appearance, the paper lining should be removed from each cupcake before it's glazed.

Note 2: This recipe makes enough glaze to coat the top and flow a bit over the sides of twelve cupcakes. Double the recipe if you want the cupcakes to be more generously coated.

Caramel icing

This isn't a neat icing: It drips over the edges of the cupcakes, necessitating extra paper liners to avoid sticky fingers. Nonetheless, the rich caramel flavor sings out.

Makes about 1¼ cups, enough for 12 cupcakes

6 tablespoons (¾ stick) unsalted
   butter
⅔ cup firmly packed dark brown
   sugar
Pinch salt

¼ cup milk
1 teaspoon pure vanilla extract
1 cup confectioners' sugar, sifted if
   lumpy

1. In a small heavy saucepan over moderate heat, melt the butter. Add the brown sugar and the salt. Cook, stirring, until the sugar melts and is incorporated into the butter.

2. Bring the mixture to a boil. Slowly pour in the milk, whisking constantly as it is added. Bring the mixture to a full rolling boil. Remove from the heat and let cool completely.

3. Transfer the caramel mixture to a medium bowl. Add the vanilla and beat until blended with an electric mixer on medium speed. Lower the mixer speed to low. Gradually add

the sugar, beating well after each addition. Continue beating until the icing becomes thick and fluffy.

4. Dip and twirl cupcakes in the icing. Let them stand until the icing is set, then dip again, adding any decorations, such as whole nuts, before the icing sets again.

5. For a neat presentation, place the decorated cupcakes in fresh paper liners.

CHOCOLATE SATIN GLAZE

This glaze's elegant sheen makes it a natural topping for Chocolate-Walnut Cupcakes.

Makes about 1½ cups, enough for 12 cupcakes

⅔ cup heavy or whipping cream

2 bars (3 ounces each) bittersweet or semisweet chocolate, chopped

2 tablespoons unsalted butter

2 tablespoons light corn syrup

In a small heavy saucepan over moderately low heat, bring the cream to a boil. Remove from the heat. Add the chocolate, butter, and corn syrup, shaking the pan to immerse the chocolate in the hot cream. Let stand for 1 minute, then beat vigorously with a wire whisk.

VARIATION

If desired, 1 tablespoon of liqueur or strong coffee may be added to the glaze just before it's beaten with the whisk.

MANGO COULIS

Served with Coconut Macaroon Cupcakes, this brightly colored sauce looks smashing on a plate, whether used alone or in combination with raspberry purée.

Makes about 1½ cups, enough for 12 cupcakes

3 large ripe mangoes (about 1½ pounds), peeled, pitted, and cut up
2 tablespoons fresh orange juice
1 tablespoon fresh lemon juice

1 tablespoon white rum or orange liqueur
1 tablespoon sugar

1. Place the mango pieces, orange and lemon juices, rum, and sugar in the work bowl of a food processor. Process until smooth and well blended.

2. Strain the sauce through a fine sieve into a medium bowl. (This removes the mango strings.) Cover and refrigerate until serving time.

MICROWAVE FUDGE SAUCE

To make miniature ice-cream cakes, use this quick-fix sauce to top cupcakes that have been sandwiched with tiny scoops of ice cream. Once prepared, the sauce can be reheated in its container in the microwave.

Makes about 2½ cups, enough for 12 cupcakes.

½ pound semisweet chocolate, chopped
1 square (1 ounce) unsweetened chocolate, quartered
⅔ cup heavy or whipping cream
⅓ cup firmly packed light brown sugar

⅓ cup light corn syrup
¼ cup (½ stick) unsalted butter
1 tablespoon instant espresso powder
Pinch salt
2 tablespoons rum
1 teaspoon pure vanilla extract

1. Combine all of the ingredients except the rum and vanilla in an 8-cup glass measure or bowl.

2. Microwave on high for 2 minutes. Stir. Continue microwaving on high for 1 to 3 minutes longer, stirring after each minute, or until the sauce is smooth and thick.

3. Stir in the rum and vanilla.

4. Store any leftover sauce in a glass jar. To reheat the sauce, remove the lid and microwave on high for 1 minute.

VARIATION

Chocolate-Orange Sauce: Substitute 2 tablespoons of orange liqueur for the rum and add 1 teaspoon grated orange zest.

CARAMEL-COFFEE-
NUT SAUCE

Serve this transparent sauce over cupcakes that have been split and filled with ice cream. Good combinations include Hot-Milk Sponge Cakes with coffee ice cream, Devil's Food Cupcakes with vanilla ice cream, and Caramel Cupcakes with chocolate ice cream.

Makes about 2 cups, enough for 12 cupcakes

¼ cup water
1 cup sugar
⅓ cup strong brewed coffee
⅔ cup heavy or whipping cream
½ teaspoon fresh lemon juice

2 tablespoons Kahlúa or other coffee
 liqueur
½ cup toasted chopped almonds,
 macadamia nuts, or cashews

1. Place the water in a small heavy saucepan. Add the sugar and let stand until the sugar is wet. Place the saucepan over moderately high heat.

2. Cook, swirling the pan occasionally, until the mixture turns nut-brown. Watch for burning. Remove the saucepan from the heat.

3. Averting your face to avoid splatters, slowly pour the coffee, then the cream, into the saucepan. Return the saucepan to the heat and continue cooking, stirring constantly, until the caramel melts into the coffee. Remove from the heat and cool.

4. Stir the lemon juice and liqueur into the sauce. Just before serving, stir in the toasted nuts.

SPIRITED WHITE-CHOCOLATE CREAM

This light filling, which can be varied by changing the liqueur you add to it, is delicious when piped into the middle of Devil's Food Cupcakes. Each cupcake can also be topped with a rosette of the cream. The cassis produces an appealing lavender color.

Makes about 1⅓ cups, enough for 12 cupcakes

¼ cup (1½ ounces) white-chocolate pieces or half of a 3-ounce bar, broken into pieces
¾ cup heavy or whipping cream

1 tablespoon sugar
1 tablespoon raspberry, orange, apricot, or cassis liqueur

1. Place the white-chocolate pieces, ¼ cup, of the cream, and the sugar in a small heat-proof bowl or the top of a double boiler.

2. Place over a pot of hot, not boiling, water. Heat, stirring occasionally, until the choco-

late is melted and the mixture is smooth. Remove from the heat; stir in the liqueur. Cool for 10 minutes.

3. In a small bowl with an electric mixer on high speed, beat the remaining ½ cup of cream until stiff peaks form. Fold the cream into the melted chocolate mixture.

CANNOLI FILLING/ TOPPING

This ricotta, fruit, and chocolate mixture can be spread in the middle of split cupcakes, or it can be used as a topping. If you're not a fan of candied orange or lemon peel, reduce it or eliminate it altogether and increase the raisins and cherries accordingly.

Makes about 1¼ cups, enough to frost or fill 12 cupcakes

1 tablespoon dried cherries
1 tablespoon raisins
2 teaspoons candied lemon and/or orange peel, rinsed and drained
1 tablespoon orange liqueur or rum

1 cup fresh ricotta cheese
2 tablespoons sugar
¼ cup miniature semisweet chocolate pieces

1. In a small bowl, combine the dried cherries, raisins, orange and/or lemon peel, and orange liqueur. Cover and let stand for at least 1 hour.

2. Place the ricotta in the work bowl of a food processor or the container of a blender. Cover and process until smooth, stopping the motor once or twice to scrape down the

sides of the work bowl or container. With the motor running, add the sugar through the feed tube.

3. Stop the motor. Add the fruit-liqueur mixture and the chocolate pieces. (Replace the plunger to the processor tube, as the mixture is likely to splash.) Cover and process with on-off pulses until blended.

4. Scrape and pour the mixture into a small bowl. It will be quite liquidy but will firm up when refrigerated. Cover lightly and refrigerate several hours or overnight to set. Keep refrigerated until you use it.

Finishing Flourishes

ecorative garnishes add the last, and perhaps most personal, touch to cupcakes. They can be as simple as a candied cherry or a sprinkling of jimmies. Or they can be more fanciful—rosettes of buttercream, marzipan fruits, whole candied nuts. This chapter includes ideas for a whole range of decorations and finishes.

BAKING—BEYOND THE BASICS

• Bake cupcakes in pans with unusual shapes—such as hearts, shells, animals, or eggs—which you can find in cookware shops. The yields and baking times will probably differ, so the cupcakes must be watched more closely while they bake.

• Bake cupcakes in flat-bottomed ice-cream cones: Place each cone on a baking sheet. Fill the cones two-thirds full with batter and bake as usual. Frost the

cooled cupcakes and garnish with the same trimmings used for ice-cream cones, such as chocolate jimmies and rainbow sprinkles. (Great for kids!)

VARIATIONS ON A THEME

• Wrap baked cupcakes in terra cotta–colored marzipan; add a rim of marzipan around the top of each cupcake to make a flowerpot. Fill with chocolate frosting, to make the soil. Insert a flower, either real or artificial, in each cupcake. (If the flower is real, be sure to wrap the stem well in aluminum foil or plastic wrap so that none of the stem touches the cake or frosting.)

• Make "butterflies": Cut off the top fourth of each cupcake and cut each top in half. Generously frost the cupcakes and insert the halves at an angle, to simulate the wings of a butterfly.

• Make fruit shortcakes from cupcakes, whipped cream, and fresh fruit, arranged in the same manner as a biscuit shortcake.

• Bake cupcakes of contrasting colors and flavors. Cut them vertically in half. Rejoin with frosting or jam, using half of each type of cupcake. Frost and garnish as usual.

• Split cupcakes and fill with ice cream. Serve with Coffee-Caramel-Nut Sauce or Microwave Fudge Sauce.

• Remove paper liners from cupcakes, if used. Roll the cupcakes in Billowy Frosting, then in coconut, to make snowballs.

FUN WITH FROSTING

• Tint buttercream two colors. Marbleize the buttercream on top of the cupcakes by swirling the colors together with a butter knife. Or, frost half of the cupcake with one color, the other with the second color, for a harlequin effect.

- Swirl the frosting in a spiral.
- Use Black-and-White Glaze, to make a cupcake version of the popular jumbo cookie.
- Top frosted cupcakes with a rosette of frosting in a contrasting flavor and color.

GREAT GARNISHES

The cupcakes are baked, the frosting's decoratively swirled. Now it's time to get creative! Because each cupcake is small, even one perfect berry or rosette of beautifully tinted frosting will lend a dramatic touch. The following ideas are meant to inspire you to create your own personal garnishes.

HOLIDAYS
New Year's Eve/Day

- Top frosted cupcakes with gold- or silver-leaf pieces (obtainable from cake-decorating supply stores or Indian food shops).
- Top frosted cupcakes with purchased chocolate bells or other seasonal chocolate shapes.
- Sprinkle silver or gold shot and multicolored coarse sugar on top of frosted cupcakes.
- Shape tiny champagne bottles and glasses from gumdrops or marzipan.

President's Day

- Make a licorice hatchet, using licorice shoelace as the handle and a cut swizzle stick as the blade.
- Make a branch of a cherry tree: Use cinnamon red hots as the cherries and licorice shoelace as the branches. Add green marzipan leaves.

Valentine's Day

- Top cupcakes with heart-shaped "conversation candy."
- Roll out pink or red gumdrops; cut into heart shapes. Place on top of frosted cupcakes, adding arrows made from licorice shoelace.
- Frost cupcakes with pink frosting, then sprinkle with red sugar.
- Top each cupcake with a chocolate heart.
- Cut maraschino cherries in half. Shape each half into a heart and place on top of frosted cupcake.

St. Patrick's Day

- Top cupcakes with shamrocks made from green gumdrops or marzipan.
- Pipe out shamrocks from green-tinted frosting.

Easter

- Top cupcakes with coconut that's been tinted green. Fill the centers of these "Easter baskets" with jelly beans.
- Top cupcakes with chocolate chicks and/or bunnies.
- Make Easter hats from marshmallows placed on small cookies; decorate with icing flowers; place on top of cupcakes.
- Top cupcakes with Easter eggs made from marzipan. Paint on decorations with food coloring.

Fourth of July

- Pipe out blue stripes on white-frosted cupcakes. Center a red raspberry or tiny red frosting rosette atop each.
- Pipe out a circle of Vanilla Whipped Cream around the top perimeter of each cupcake. Fill with blueberries and raspberries.

Halloween

- Frightful Faces: Top cupcakes with Butterscotch Frosting or Vanilla Buttercream tinted orange. Decorate with witch or black-cat faces.
- Pumpkin Patches: Top cupcakes with Vanilla Buttercream. Pipe out rosettes of orange frosting, to look like piles of pumpkins; add thin swirls of green to simulate the vines.
- Ghosts: Top cupcakes with a generous swirl of Billowy Frosting or Sweetened Whipped Cream. Add two dots of dark frosting for eyes.
- Sprinkle frosting with orange- and black-tinted sugar.
- Top cupcakes with marzipan pumpkins.

Christmas

- Fashion holly berries and leaves from colored marzipan.
- Make Christmas trees from Andes mints cut on the diagonal, the two triangles placed together at an angle.
- Top each cupcake with a chocolate-mint bell or other Christmas-motif chocolate.
- Sprinkle the frosting with red and green sugar.

VERY SIMPLE GARNISH IDEAS (FOR FROSTED CUPCAKES)

Single berries
Single nuts, plain or dipped in caramelized sugar
Sugared cranberries
Chocolate-covered coffee beans or plain coffee beans
Crushed peanut brittle
Crushed peppermint candy
M&M's
Orange- or lemon-rind shapes

Rosettes of a frosting in a contrasting color

Maraschino cherries with the stems left on

Marrons Glacés

Confectioners' sugar dusted through a small doily (only good for darkly frosted cupcakes)

Cocoa dusted through a small doily (only good for cupcakes frosted with a light buttercream)

"Daisy" made from dried apricot pieces

Small sparklers

Small paper umbrellas (great for bridal and baby showers)

Candied flowers

Fresh edible flowers

Individual chocolates

Tinted coconut

Rainbow or other colored sugar

Chocolate or rainbow sprinkles

Marzipan shapes—fruits, vegetables, animals

Lightly cover one side of the top of a frosted cupcake with a piece of heavy paper cut into the shape of a crescent moon; dust the other side with confectioners' sugar, or cocoa. Add "stars" of frosting to the undusted side.

Birthday candles in *each* cupcake make everyone feel special!

JUST FOR THE KIDS

- Top cupcakes with teddy-bear graham crackers.
- Top cupcakes with animal crackers.
- Top chocolate-frosted cupcakes with "gardens" of "dirt" made from chocolate cookie crumbs, and gardening tools, watering cans, and flowers made from marzipan.

- Top frosted cupcakes with a "seashore" of graham-cracker-crumb "sand" and candy shells.
- Top white-frosted cupcakes with "seams" of Squiggly Frosting, to make baseballs. (Or tint the frosting orange and use melted chocolate for the seams, to make basketballs.)
- Use tubes of ready-made frosting to write a letter on each cupcake, to spell out messages such as "Happy Birthday!"

SUPER SHAPES

- Marzipan or almond paste, tinted with food coloring, can be used to create all sorts of fanciful shapes and figures.
- Gumdrops are easy to work with as a modeling clay and come in lovely colors: Roll them out on a work surface using a rolling pin. Cut with tiny canapé cutters, or mold/roll into flowers and other shapes.

Index

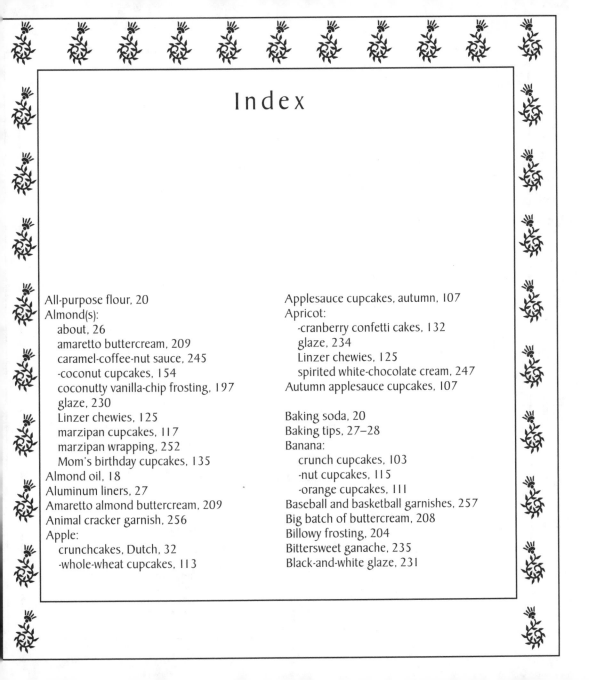

DATE			

BAKER & TAYLOR